WORKING
· WITH ·
HORSES

WORKING
· WITH ·
HORSES

Vanessa Britton

Foreword by John Goldsmith, B.H.S.

WARD LOCK

*This book is dedicated to Rhyan and Kimberly,
who have already taken their first steps into the
horse world with Chuckles and Harvey.*

First published in Great Britain in 1992
by Ward Lock Limited, Villiers House,
41/47 Strand, London WC2N 5JE, England

A Cassell imprint

Cataloguing in Publication Data available from the British Library

ISBN 0-7063-7068-6

Text filmset by Chapterhouse, Formby, L37 3PX
Printed and bound in Great Britain
by Mackays Limited, Chatham

Contents

Acknowledgements

My grateful thanks to: all of the colleges, training centres and associations listed, especially Phil Gulliver, Course Director, Norfolk College of Agriculture and Horticulture, for help with a last-minute photo-session; Mr P. Cook, head of equine and veterinary nursing studies, Bicton College of Agriculture, for putting valuable college slides at my disposal; Linda Barr of the Limbury Stud for her letter written at 5am!; Judy Mead, professional affairs officer of the Chartered Society of Physiotherapy; the Association of British Riding Schools, the British Driving Society and their junior commissioner, Mrs Caroline Dale-Leech, The National Pony Society, the Riding for the Disabled Association and the Jockey Club for providing me with and allowing me to use certain information. I am also especially grateful to John Goldsmith, Executive Officer, Training and Examinations of the British Horse Society, for providing information about the National Vocational Qualifications so promptly and for authorizing me to use information as I so wished. Many thanks also to Paul Smith for supplying illustrations.

I would also like to give a mention to Janet Turner of the Crofts Stud, who has given freely her help and knowledge in stud practice and showing, and has had her ear bashed ever since!

Finally, all of the employers who answered my questionnaire, too many to mention by name, so thank you one and all.

Foreword

It is only in recent years that the existence of a horse industry in UK has been recognised. The British Horse Society's study 'The Economic Contribution of the British Equine Industry' carried out by Peat, Marwick, McLintock in 1988 indicated that almost 100,000 people are employed in the industry.

This book provides a fund of information on the major employment sectors of the industry and valuable guidance for those considering a career working in the horse industry. There has been a need for a comprehensive guide for some time and those who give career advice (in my own case to several thousand enquiries each year) will welcome publication of *Working With Horses* by Vanessa Britton.

John Goldsmith, BHS

Introduction

So you like horses! Well, good for you, but take a closer look. Do you really want to work with them?

'It's just a phase you'll probably grow out of when you get a bit older'. I wish that I had a pound for every time I was told that. 'Not me!' I hear you cry. Well, read on; you are just the type of person this book is for.

I was not born into a horsey family, and did not know a head from a tail until I was 9 years old. However, once the bug bit me, I was determined to learn. At my local riding school that was exactly what I was told, and learn I did, my visions of grandeur soon diminished.

From when I was very young, I expect like a lot of you, I had an uncontrollable love for horses. At first it was just a dream. Reading books; catching every snippet of information about those creatures so strong and bold, yet so calm and collected.

Then suddenly, before you know what has hit you, the dream is reality and you are living, breathing and sleeping horses.

I hope to help you through this transition, from those of you who are thinking about careers at middle-school level, to people of all ages who are new to the world of equestrianism.

I am aiming at people from all walks of life, whether they have been involved with horses before or not. The principles could as well be applied by adults or children alike planning their futures.

I cannot guarantee that if you follow these principles you will gain employment, but you will be presenting yourself to potential employers in a responsible and professional way.

Horsemanship is a very satisfying occupation, you will not only be fulfilled by gaining employment, you will also be getting job satisfaction; acquiring more knowledge as you continue on your chosen path.

You will be learning a trade – as in any other job. However, should you discover along the way that a groom's life is not quite the life you wanted, then help is at hand. I hope to give an insight into other related industries, not necessarily involved with the everyday management of horses. Providing ideas other than those most commonly thought of by people wishing to join the industry themselves.

Although you may be attracted to a career with horses, it would be

CAREER PATHS

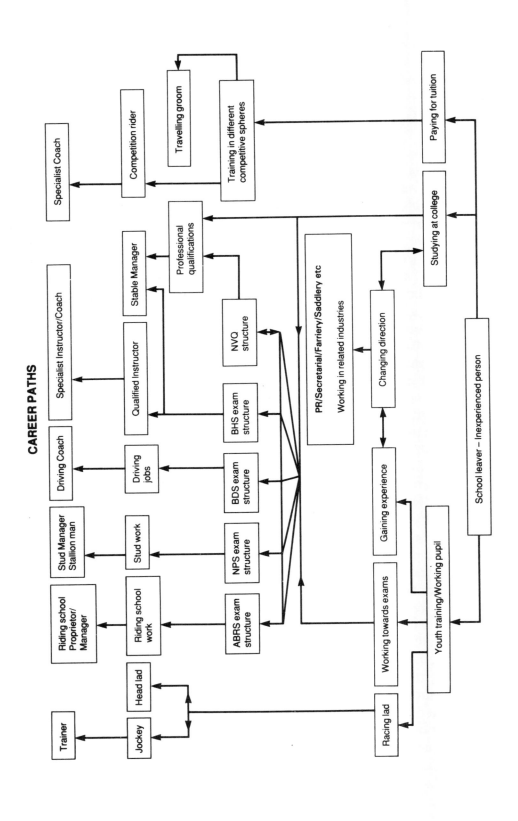

foolish to continue with any form of training, unless you also have a real love for them, and are prepared for many dedicated, hard-working years ahead. Every horse is an individual character, so each needs kind, firm, but understanding handling.

To find a decent job in the future, you will need practical experience. You may learn theoretical knowledge from reading text books, but there really is no alternative to practical training.

Recognized qualifications are what are needed for today's standards. The prospects for those who are professionally trained are good, as the horse industry in general is flourishing. In particular, good grooms are difficult to find, therefore trained, experienced grooms can now choose a position to suit them. The traditional attitudes of employers, that grooms must be prepared for long hours, hard often dirty work and low wages are being fought by grooms who expect acceptable wages, conditions and accommodation. Grooms have a right to expect this for their years spent training and gaining experience, often in less than satisfactory conditions.

The most important thing -- not to be forgotten, is that you must be dedicated to horses and their care. The work is more a way of life than simply a job.

Progression with qualifications and experience is possible throughout the industry. This not only helps grooms with chances for promotion but also helps employers to find and retain good grooms at the level of employment offered, with the knowledge that they can be relied upon to do their job properly.

Until now work with horses has been treated as an extension to one's *hobbies*, but with the new education structures coming into force, which have to be in line with the Single European Market opening up in 1992, the whole industry can command a wholly *professional* status.

My advice to you is to get yourself qualified, get as much practical experience as you can, then go out and find yourself a lasting, fulfilling career.

WHAT JOB DO I WANT?

When you first leave school or first look at the equestrian industry with a view to employment, you may be a little confused as to just where you want to go. Some of you may already have experience with horses and may have gained an insight into a particular area that interests you. However, those of you who have no idea need not despair, for all you need to do is ask yourself a few questions. Answer them truthfully and you will be guiding yourself along a path which should lead to the job best suited to your interests and personality.

This book will help you to solve the question, in which part of the industry you would like to work, very easily. Firstly, study the *career path questions* and answer them to the best of your ability. Do not fall into the trap of answering them with a particular job area in mind or you may lead yourself up the wrong path. Once you have established the career area with which your answers correspond, turn to that particular section to find out more. The 'Structure of Career Paths' diagram will also aid your search. Start at the bottom and follow the routes you would like to take to see where they can lead. For example: did you know that studying for the National Pony Society (NPS) examinations could lead you into a job as a stud manager or stallion man?

You will also see that the diagram allows you to change direction if you decide that you want to pursue other possibilities. You will see that you cannot go from studying British Horse Society (BHS) exams to becoming a driving coach; for that would not be possible within the industry itself unless you went back and studied for the British Driving Society (BDS) examinations.

So, the 'Structure of Career Paths' diagram acts as a quick reference to possible career paths; the career path questions make you think about what area might suit you, and the sections and chapters of the book go on to explain the type of work involved in such different areas. Once you have read the book you should be clear in your mind which career path you would like to follow.

Career path 1

1	Do I mind if I am not able to ride?	yes / no
2	Do I mind not earning lots of money?	yes / no
3	Do I mind working in all weathers?	yes / no
4	Do I mind not having much time off, if necessary?	yes / no
5	Am I good at taking orders?	yes / no
6	Am I going to be punctual, tidy and hard-working?	yes / no
7	Can I manage the physical aspects of the work?	yes / no
8	Do I get on well with children and other people?	yes / no
9	Would I like to study for qualifications?	yes / no
10	Will I put the care of horses in my charge first?	yes / no

If you answered no to 1–4 and yes to 5–10 then a job in a *riding school* or *livery yard* might suit you. Turn to the section on *livery yards* and *riding schools* (Chapter 2) and then to Youth Training (Chapter 5) to find out more.

Career path 2

1 Am I dedicated to following the BHS exam structure?	yes / no
2 Can I give orders and speak with authority?	yes / no
3 Can I instil confidence in others?	yes / no
4 Do I get on well with both adults and children?	yes / no
5 Do I keep myself smart and tidy?	yes / no
6 Do I have plenty of patience?	yes / no
7 Do I like organizing things?	yes / no
8 Do I have any competitive ambitions?	yes / no
9 Do I panic when things go wrong?	yes / no
10 Do I want to have set holidays and days off?	yes / no
11 Do I want to travel?	yes / no

If you answered yes to 1–7 and no to 8–11 then a job as a *riding school instructor* may suit you. Turn to the sections on following the *BHS examination structure* (Chapter 5) to see if you can stay the course.

Career path 3

1 Do I want to travel?	yes / no
2 Am I able to work on my own initiative?	yes / no
3 Do I like preparing horses for shows?	yes / no
4 Will I be loyal to my employer?	yes / no
5 Do I mind getting up very early?	yes / no
6 Do I mind not knowing what tomorrow will bring?	yes / no
7 Do I mind staying at home while others are competing?	yes / no
8 Do I mind putting horses and riders before myself?	yes / no
9 Do I mind staying away from home?	yes / no
10 Would I like the chance to compete?	yes / no

If you answered yes to 1–4 and no to 5–9 then a job in a *competition yard* might suit you. The choice of which competitive sphere you prefer is up to you so turn to Chapter 2 to see what interests you most. If you answered yes to question 10, you should find out from a potential employer whether you will have a chance to compete at some stage, as someone with competitive ambitions might find the work frustrating if there are no opportunties to compete, or even ride.

Career path 4

1	Am I able to work in isolation?	yes / no
2	Can I work quickly and efficiently?	yes / no
3	Can I get up very early and work before breakfast?	yes / no
4	Can I keep my weight down?	yes / no
5	Can I take orders and act on them exactly?	yes / no
6	Do I mind travelling with horses?	yes / no
7	Do I want a normal social life?	yes / no
8	Do I panic when things start to get hectic?	yes / no
9	Do highly strung horses make me nervous?	yes / no
10	Would I like the opportunity of racing one day?	yes / no

If you answered yes to 1–5 and no to 6–9 than a career in the *racing industry* might suit you very well, either as a stable lad or as an apprentice jockey. If you answered yes to question 10 then you will have to become an apprentice jockey and work very hard indeed. Turn to the section on *racing* (Chapter 2) to find out more.

Career path 5

1	Would I mind studying at college?	yes / no
2	Am I prepared to put in many years of hard work in both the practical and theoretical aspects of the industry?	yes / no
3	Am I a natural leader?	yes / no
4	Am I good at delegating?	yes / no
5	Can I be diplomatic?	yes / no
6	Can I get on with anyone?	yes / no
7	Can I give orders sympathetically?	yes / no
8	Can I listen objectively to other people's opinions?	yes / no
9	Can I create enthusiasm in others?	yes / no
10	Do I find there are never enough hours in the day?	yes / no

If you answered no to 1 and yes to all the others then you would possibly be suited to a *managerial position* or *self employment*. Turn to the section on *managerial positions* (Chapter 2) and then to the chapter on running a business (Chapter 3) to see if that is where your future lies.

Career path 6

1 Do I have some experience with horses but do not actually want to look after their physical, day-to-day needs? — yes / no
2 Am I a good thinker? — yes / no
3 Am I good at paperwork? — yes / no
4 Am I able to follow my own ideas through? — yes / no
5 Do I enjoy talking to equestrian people? — yes / no
6 Am I able to speak clearly and knowledgeably? — yes / no
7 Am I good at writing with flair? — yes / no
8 Am I good at making things? — yes / no
9 Would I like to work for myself one day? — yes / no
10 Am I prepared for further training? — yes / no

If you answered yes to most of the questions then your career path might take you into a related industry such as *public relations, farriery, saddlery* or *secretarial work* within horse organizations. Turn to Chapter 4 to see what is involved in such jobs and which one might suit you best.

While this book is intended to give you all available information on career paths open to you, and so covers all available options through the BHS, ABRS, NPS, BDS and so on, this should be seen in the light that the BHS is the major equestrian examination force worldwide. In 1991 over 11,500 people took their professional examinations from all over the world. Also, in the $3\frac{1}{2}$ years that the BHS has been running progressive riding tests, more than 20,000 people have taken them.

There are about 650 BHS approved centres in Great Britain and these are inspected annually by nationally recognised individuals, who are totally independent of the BHS and who arrive unannounced.

1

While still at school

The first decision you will have to make if you want to pursue a career with horses will be what exams to take to help you in the future. In addition, you should have something to fall back on in case you later decide that the horse world as a means of employment is not for you. Maths and English are a must. Passes in such subjects as biology, environmental studies and any agricultural sciences that are available would be an advantage. You should, however, take into account that you are more likely to pass in the subjects that you are interested in, than those where you have to really slog just to scrape through. A pass in any subject is better than a failure in one relevant to the horse world.

You may be lucky enough to attend a school that offers a General Certificate of Education (GCSE) Mode 3 Horsemastership course. This is run by the Southern Examining Group and is designed to provide you with the opportunity to gain knowledge and awareness of the horse.

This qualification will enable you to develop a leisure pursuit, provide a basis for entering into the horse industry and a foundation for further study. A pass in this subject will give you an advantage when starting out in the horse industry.

WORKING WITH HORSES: CAREER OR HOBBY?

Having made your educational choices, which at this stage are your first priority, you can begin to think about where your future lies. You have three main options regarding the form that your involvement will take. Firstly, you might not want to be employed in the industry at all. You may decide to keep your horse interests as a hobby, working full-time in another line of business altogether. Secondly, you may decide that you only want to work with horses part-time; for example, after qualifying as an instructor, you may want to do some freelance teaching on weekends and evenings, yet pursue full-time employment in a different industry. Lastly, your future hopes may be totally set on pursuing a full-time career with horses.

These options may be a long way off for those of you still at school, but the importance of planning ahead at this stage cannot be stressed enough.

WAYS OF HELPING YOURSELF

■ *Helping at a local riding school*
There are various ways of gaining experience with horses before leaving school, and a good one is to ask at your local riding school whether they need helpers at weekends. Helpers in riding schools are commonplace nowadays; most start at an early age. Many young people acquire their first interest in a career with horses in this way, and the experience will give you a taste of what to expect when you start work *officially*.

You will be expected to join in all of the normal duties of the yard, which will include such things as mucking out, sweeping up and filling water buckets and haynets when required. Do anything you are asked willingly, quickly and without any fuss.

One of your main duties will probably be as a leader for an individual horse or pony, assisting the instructors in their lessons. Your job is to inspire some confidence in both rider and horse. Your presence will be appreciated, as without helpers the instructor would have additional problems.

Because you are helping out, it will not necessarily follow that you will be allowed to ride. However, your time will come. Be patient and you may in time earn free rides when the ponies are not being worked too hard.

The advantage of helping out at riding schools and livery yards is that there is always something going on. You can learn a great deal at this early stage if you keep your eyes and ears open. It is a good thing to ask questions, but always choose a time when the person you wish to speak to is not busy.

If the riding school holds lectures and demonstrations, you should try to attend. The more you can learn at this stage, when you are not tied to any particular area of equestrianism, the better. You will be helping yourself to widen your options, and starting to close doors on subjects that do not seem to interest you. However, do not rule out anything completely, for things that do not interest you at the present time may seem more attractive when you have more knowledge and experience. For example, you might not be interested in driving, but should you outgrow a family pony, you can still keep it in active work if you teach it to drive.

The marks of a good helper are: punctuality; cleanliness and tidiness; observation; politeness; willingness to work; and above all, a sense of responsibility.

Stable Helpers' Certificate

This is run and encouraged by the Association of British Riding Schools (ABRS). An ABRS Stable Helpers' Certificate may be awarded to those helpers who prove themselves capable and reliable. The object of this examination is to encourage young people to gain a wider knowledge of the workings of a riding establishment, that they may become valuable helpers who are well grounded and prepared for further training.

To be eligible you must be a minimum of 14 years old, and have helped at or attended an ABRS school for a minimum of 1 year. You may be examined at the school you attend, during a normal working day.

For a syllabus you should apply to: The General Secretary, Association of British Riding Schools (see Appendix). An enclosed stamped addressed envelope will speed up the reply considerably.

■ *Livery yards*

You may find livery-yard proprietors a little more reluctant to take up your offer of help. Most of the horses will belong to clients, who are paying for their horses to be looked after by experienced grooms. The management is held responsible should anything happen to the horses in their care. Some animals may be valuable competition horses, and owners could be very annoyed to learn that people other than experienced grooms were looking after their animals. This opinion is very understandable; they have every right to expect only the best of care, and the owners' wishes must be respected at all times.

There are ways of working around these problems. You can volunteer to do the menial tasks such as mucking out and cleaning tack – jobs that do not actually involve handling the horses but are an essential part of the smooth running of the yard. Once you have shown that you are a responsible, hard-working person, they may be prepared to let you groom and help with the horses while under close supervision.

■ *Owning/sharing a pony*

Some of you may be lucky enough to own your own ponies or horses already, and will be learning new things all the time. If you do not own a pony or live near enough to a riding school, you could try approaching a friend who has one. Should your parents be able to afford it, or you earn your own money from a part-time job, you may be able to share a pony with a friend.

Horses cost a lot of money to keep, and ownership should not be a decision taken lightly. You must be sure that you can take care of a horse 7 days a week, 52 weeks a year. A total commitment is needed; any less will not do. Horses expect to be fed every day, including Christmas Day and any other occasion.

If you find yourself in a position where you do have access to a horse, make the most of it. Do not ride unless you have the time to muck-out and groom afterwards, better to give a good groom and forget the ride altogether. A horse's happiness must come before your own pleasure. They did not ask to be domesticated, and the least we can do is to make sure that they are well cared for.

The advantage of being able to deal with a certain horse on a one-to-one basis is that you can build up a relationship with a particular animal, getting to know its habits, likes and dislikes. Experiences like this are invaluable. It will help you to appreciate their true worth. They can become your best friend or your worst enemy, the choice is yours.

It is essential that you realize at an early age, whether you think you can cope with the physical side of looking after horses. If you do not think that you can, it would be far better to find out sooner than later. You could then pursue another career, yet still keep horses and riding as a hobby, paying for lessons or going out for enjoyable hacks.

■ *The Pony Club*

Your pony years could be some of your most enjoyable, especially if you belong to the Pony Club (see p. 120). The Pony Club is for all young riders who share a love for horses and ponies. You do not have to own a pony to be a member. All Pony Club members ride and are keen to improve their knowledge of both riding and how to care for horses and ponies properly.

Pony Club test standards

Every member has an opportunity to qualify for one of the coveted proficiency certificates. These cover such subjects as; stable management, road safety, country lore, horsemanship and riding ability. Standards of efficiency range from the D test, which is a basic test of ability, up to the top standard test of A. There are also an H Horsemastership Test and Countryside Awards, which you can work towards obtaining.

■ *Paying for tuition*

At certain riding schools, you can pay to go on courses for riding and stable management before you leave school. These courses will probably take the form of a couple of hours riding, both hacking and tuition, the rest of the time being taken up with normal stable duties, including such things as tack cleaning, grooming and mucking-out. These courses are usually run in school holidays and as such are normally called holiday courses.

Even if you own a pony or have access to one, you will still benefit from any of these ideas. You cannot learn the practical requirements of a groom from the experience with one pony alone – or from a book; unless, of course, your parents or family are well experienced in horse management and are prepared to teach you. You would probably be welcome to take your own pony along, having made prior arrangements with the riding school.

Should you decide to try one of these courses, you should first make sure that you go to a riding or equitation centre that has a good reputation, even if it is not the nearest one. You should make sure that:

- The staff are qualified to teach.
- You will be supervized at all times.
- You are not being charged extortionate fees.
- Ask how many with you on the course.
- How many teachers to the number of pupils.
- What range of subjects will be taught.
- How many hours you will be actively engaged.

- What provisions are made for lunch if staying all day.

You are paying, so you are entitled to the proper service. Should you find that the people concerned are not willing to answer your questions when you go to have a look around, find a centre that is. While you are there, look at the state of the horses: do they appear well fed and looked after? Are the staff cheerful and helpful? Is everywhere clean and tidy? These points will give you a good indication as to whether you will be learning the correct things in a happy atmosphere. The latter is very important. It is much easier to learn if you feel happy and relaxed. It becomes a drudge if you are fed up and bored.

It is a good idea to take a short course like this to compliment your weekly or fortnightly riding. You will need to know all aspects of stable management before anyone would consider you as a work rider, just to exercise their horses. Practical experience in any form is a better advantage from an employer's point of view, especially if you are a school-leaver. The time that you have between school hours is very valuable – use it wisely. After attending such a course, you may be awarded with a certificate from the school.

Your best approach is to go to a BHS (British Horse Society) or an ABRS (Association of British Riding Schools) approved centre, as they have been tested in the required disciplines up to a very high standard. You should apply to the BHS and ABRS secretaries for a list of approved centres (see Appendix). Enclose a stamped addressed envelope and you should have no problems.

TEST OPTIONS

At this stage, before you leave school, there are some test options open to you. These are designed to give you an encouraging start with horse work and riding.

■ ABRS Equitation Tests for Weekly Riders

The object of these tests, which range from Test 0 to Test 10, is to prove that the weekly rider has reached a recognized standard of competence in equitation. The ultimate aim is that you are able to ride an elementary dressage test, and also to ride a variety of horses in the open, on the flat and over a course of varied obstacles including jumps of a height not exceeding 0.09 m (3 ft).

■ *ABRS Weekly Rider Alternative Flatwork Tests*

These tests have been devised to give riders who prefer not to jump alternative flatwork content (a basic pre-jumping test remains as a requirement).

The alternative flatwork section is applicable when taking Tests 6 to 9.

■ *ABRS Stable Management Tests*

The aims of these tests, graded from 0 to 10, are to provide nationally recognized standards of competence for those interested in the care, welfare and management of horses.

The tests mark your progress by progressive instruction and practice, and towards the end of such education you will be able to attain a reasonable standard in stable management.

■ *Bronze, Silver and Gold Awards*

Candidates who have passed Test 9 in riding and stable management will receive a Bronze Award.

Candidates who have passed Test 10 in riding and stable management will receive a Silver Award and become eligible to take the test for the Gold Award.

■ *ABRS Side-saddle Tests*

These tests are run on the same lines as the weekly riders' tests, except they cater for side-saddle riders.

You will learn such things as the history and features of varying side-saddle designs, tacking up using side-saddles, and jumping, and ultimately ride a novice-standard dressage test. You will also learn about showing horses.

For a syllabus for any of the above exams, apply to the General Secretary at the ABRS offices.

■ *Riding Clubs' Grade Tests*

These grade tests have been devised to encourage members of clubs to achieve a high standard of riding and horsemanship. Clubs that participate in these tests are affiliated to the BHS. Most clubs have a junior section catering for those between 8 and 17 years, and an adult section for those over 17 years of age.

Examinations to standards recognized by the BHS include:

- Grades I to IV
- Stable Management Phases I to III
- Stable Management Certificate
- Junior Grades I to II

■ *BHS Progressive Riding Tests*

There are 12 of these, covering both riding and stable management. They are administred by BHS-approved riding establishments and you should contact one of these for full details. Tests 1–5 cover the syllabus of the BHS Horse Knowledge and Riding Stage I, so success could be a valuable step up the ladder.

HELPING AT HORSE SHOWS AND EVENTS

This might not be commonly thought of as a usual way of gaining experience. However, there is nothing more pleasing than to watch horses in competition, knowing that you are doing your bit to help the whole event run smoothly.

The first step is to enquire at your local riding club, showjumping club or Pony Club, if they would like any help. It would be very surprising if your offer was turned down, as organizers are usually glad of any willing help they can get.

You may be asked to help the stewards in the ring by putting up the fences. This can be harder than it sounds! You have to be very quick and assemble the fences accurately when they have been knocked down. 'Four faults is all the same to a horse so he might as well make a good job of it and knock the lot flying;' this train of thought must often be in the mind of many helpers!

You could be asked to jump judge. This requires a great deal of stamina and concentration. Your head will be on the chopping block with organizers and competitors if you get it wrong.

Other duties might include helping with the catering or the car-parking, or issuing competitors' numbers and collecting them in at the end of the day. You may even be asked to help in the collecting ring, taking down numbers and informing people when it is their turn.

One last important point is to make sure that you can get home from the showground safely, as most shows carry on until very late. When all of the clearing up is done it may be quite dark, so try to arrange a lift.

THE PRICE TO PAY

I would not wish to put anyone off pursuing a career working with horses, but initially there is a price to pay. When starting out there are some things that you should take into consideration. You will at first be expected to work for a low wage (although at present an attempt is being made to create a career and wage structure for the horse industry). Only in the Thoroughbred industry is there a set minimum wage for a groom, although the Transport and General Workers' Union (TGWU) recommends employers to be guided by the agricultural wages order, based on a 40-hour week.

You will be expected to work long hours, doing a lot of physical work. Days off, if you are lucky, come few and far between. Holidays are sometimes non-existent.

Although these are generalizations (some of the more established studs and riding schools have a very good policy for days off), these conditions are fairly common for a groom. However, as long as you have suitable accommodation and enough pocket money, your early years can be very satisfying. You will be learning all the time, and the more experience you get the better your career prospects will be for the future.

As you travel further up the promotional ladder, your rewards will of course be greater. You should not only be earning more money, but you will be given more responsibility.

When you start life as a groom full time, you may find that your social life tends to die. This includes boyfriends and girlfriends. Many people who do not share your interest in horses find it hard to understand the hours and the commitment that you feel towards the job. It is a very healthy life. However, sometimes a change is as good as a rest, and other interests help to keep you fresh and interested in your work.

I hope that these points have not put you off embarking on an equestrian career. Indeed most of you do not need telling that there is another side to the glamorous sports that we see on the television.

CAREER OPTIONS

2

Grooms, instructors and riders

In all the different branches of equestrianism and all the different commercial establishments, yards vary in how they run on a day-to-day basis and on a yearly programme. In some of the big competition yards there may be horses competing all year round. There is no slack period and the daily routines for both competition and non-competition days will remain constant. In the breeding establishments or riding schools, on the other hand, the winter is usually a quieter time enabling any loose ends to be tied up and any refurbishment to be taken care of.

MANAGERIAL POSITIONS – WHERE ARE YOU HEADING?

Once you have settled in and are familiar with the running of the place, it is time to establish yourself and decide what you want to achieve in the future.

A yard is made up of managers (the thinkers) and workers (the doers). The number of staff and the structure of the yard will depend on the size of the yard and what type of yard it is. To give a few examples:

A riding and training centre catering for 500 weekly
riders, with approximately 45 school horses and ponies
might be run by the following:
Manager/Boss
1 Senior Instructor
2 Instructors
3 Trainee Instructors
5 Grooms

Taking into account that most riding schools give both horses and staff a day off each week, a yard comprised of the above should be able to run quite smoothly and safely. The horses, although some will be used more than others, depending on the riders' abilities, will be fairly worked.

A competition yard regularly competing 30 horses at all levels and bringing on 20 young horses, either for sale or competition might be run by the following:

Main Rider

2 Up-and-coming Riders

4 Schooling/work Riders

6 Grooms

A yard such as this should be a successful one, having three riders on the circuit, two or three grooms travelling with them and the rest of the staff dealing with all the work at home. As many horses will probably be sold on, this is an ever-changing scene that demands constant enthusiasm.

You will have to decide where you wish to fit in to this scene. If you are training in a riding school there may be opportunities for promotion as and when you become qualified. If there are not, you will have to move on and find a position that commands more responsibility.

If you are working as a groom in a competition yard there will be little chance of promotion unless you have very good riding ability. In this case, you may have a chance of competing on the novice horses, trying to build a reputation as an up-and-coming rider.

In a breeding establishment you can work towards becoming head lad. The positions for stallion men are few and far between. You will not only have to wait until you are considered experienced enough, but probably also until the current stallion man retires!

In the racing world you will also be aiming for the position of head lad, unless of course you are trying to pursue a career as a jockey. The requirements for this are quite clear, either you will make the grade or you will not.

If, having worked in a yard and gained much experience, you find that you are not cut out for a managerial position, you might like to try another option.

You may be able to find a job in the office of a well-established yard, where someone with first-hand knowledge and experience with horses is required. Many of these positions exist, although they are hotly contested. To deal with all the paperwork, and people such as clients and owners, needs somebody who is familiar with the correct horse terminology.

LIVERY AND RIDING CENTRES

Most opportunities for school-leavers are provided by these centres. You should have the chance to train for either the BHS, ABRS or NPS exams (see Chapter 6), whereby you will train as you work.

If there are such things as normal groom's duties, this is where they will be exercised. All of the things that you have learnt throughout your association with horses up to date will now come in useful.

Your day will start with the checking, feeding, mucking out and grooming that are general practice in all stables. Then you will probably have to help with tacking up, and leading horses for the instructor. As you become better qualified, your duties may alter, and you may also be allowed to accompany hacks. If you are training to become an instructor, you may be allowed to assist in teaching beginners until you are qualified yourself.

Once you are qualified, you may decide to stay on if there is a position for you, or you might want to find a job where you will have more responsibility, or to follow a specialist career. Either way, you will have the option of further training.

Teaching somebody else to ride is a very difficult task. You will need to show that you have acquired an enormous amount of knowledge and experience over many years, to instil confidence in others. Not only do you need a knowledge of horses and riding, but you should have an ability to understand people. As every horse is an individual, so is every human being, young or old. To get and keep a pupil's attention and co-operation you will need exemplary patience and understanding.

EVENTING

To be a successful event groom, perhaps eventually riding in events yourself, you will need your wits about you more than ever. Event grooms have to work very hard indeed. Being prepared to travel is also essential. Eventing is an international sport and travelling abroad for long periods is quite usual. Events have to be entered well in advance. It is not unusual for the following year's proposed events to be worked out directly following the results of each horse at the end of the season.

It is a very professional sport, although amateurs compete with good results against the professionals, as it is really the combination of horse, rider, groom and trainer that determines the success of each individual competitor. There is a great deal of camaraderie between all riders and grooms, the emphasis being on your own horse doing well, rather than beating the opposition.

A good groom is of valuable help during competitions. You should be aware of the time allowed for each section so that you can assist the rider at the appropriate times between phases. It is the test of a good groom to keep a horse happy, fit and sound for the final show-jumping test. The vet's inspection has become a very serious business in recent times, as awareness of the problems horses have in retaining energy and suppleness after the demanding endurance phase has greatly increased.

Vigilant, well-trained grooms will keep their charges happy by walking them out in hand, allowing them to graze on a lead, and ensuring that they get a thorough grooming to keep stiffness at bay. Happy horses win competitions, miserable ones do nothing, but at best scrape round. At times, event grooms will stay at home, helping with the essential training, grooming and exercising of the younger or unfit horses. You should be able to cope in any circumstance, showing positive, clear thinking in any action that you take.

SHOWJUMPING

Showjumping has a world-wide following of millions. It is a very big spectator sport. The thrill of the big fences and the chase against the clock in top competitions keep everybody on the edge of their seats until the very end.

With some of the top riders you could find yourself up early in the morning and dashing across country to help with horses that are jumping a few rounds. To any professional member of the show-jumping scene, every round is as important as the next. The aim is to get horses upgraded, but this cannot be achieved unless the horses win money. It takes a lot of competitions, or wins of a very high standard, before a rider can hope for his horse to reach Grade A.

Although riders on the county circuit have to enter classes months beforehand, many riders decide to enter horses in all different shows on impulse, depending on how the horse is going at the time. Such is the life of a showjumping groom that you may find yourself trying to plait up on the way to the show, or cleaning the tack in the back of the lorry.

Working for a professional showjumper can be very hectic as there are usually one, often two and maybe even three shows a week. It is a constantly changing scene, as riders pick the competitions that are best suited to the horses they are riding at the current time. Grooms are expected to organize everything that needs to be seen to, before they have to be asked to do it, and delays cannot be catered for when time is of the essence.

Again, as with all competitive sports, the standard of competition which you can hope to attend depends entirely on the riders' experience and which circuit they wish to travel round. Some prefer to stay at home on the county circuit. Those that have top-class horses like to travel on the international circuit. Some try to do both. Wherever you find yourself, at home, travelling, or abroad, the rules for the job you are doing remain the same.

You could be put in charge of quite a few horses, each one requiring the same treatment, which may involve exercising. As with all horse sports many horses are left at home, consequently you may have to stay home and look after them. There is a lot of work that needs to be done in training. It involves a lot of practise and a fair bit of your time could be used in putting up fences. If you are lucky, you may get tuition in showjumping, progressing if you are good enough to riding the novices in small competitions.

A good showjumping groom can make all the difference to the success of the team. Each horse's overall performance will be affected by his daily management and care. Showjumpers need to be kept calm in all situations, at all times, as many of the top competitions are run at irregular intervals. This is your department. Horse and groom need to build a good relationship, trusting each other entirely. This will help you to get the horse in the right place at the right time, in the right frame of mind to do the best it can. Your job is to help relieve some of the pressures on the rider/owner by doing your job efficiently and effectively.

DRESSAGE

The sport of dressage needs extreme dedication. Hours of practice are put in by riders trying to obtain the exact movement required for each stage of the horse's development.

The aim is to upgrade the horses, although the system works on points obtained rather than money. The scale of points is the same for all affiliated competitions and ranges from seven points for first, down to one point for seventh in the summer competitions, and three points for first, to one point for third in the winter competitions.

Competitors can phone up to obtain their approximate starting times. This is a big help to both rider and groom as you will know roughly when to set out from home and everything can be prepared in advance. Both horse and rider have to be immaculate, presentation and the overall look of the combination being very important. A good impression created before the start makes the judges sit up and watch.

It is essential for a dressage groom to have plenty of patience. Hours and hours are put in to get the horses looking and performing their best. Horses undergo a lot of road work and schooling exercises to keep them in the peak condition that is needed. A very calm overall outlook is needed if the team is to be a success.

THE TRAVELLING GROOM

Good travelling grooms are worth their weight in gold. Anybody who travels horses to competitions regularly will confirm this without having to think about it. As well as having to see that everything runs as smoothly as possible, the travelling groom must help to relieve some of the pressures on the rider.

When an employer thinks about finding the right person for the job, he/she is almost certainly going to pick the most reliable person they know. This person may not have an outstanding ability in every aspect of horse management, but he/she knows that they will get the job done correctly with the minimum of fuss. Above all they will always be there, through successes and failures, keeping their cool.

An employer, which in this case is usually a professional rider or trainer or occasionally an owner, is likely to examine all of the general grooms in his yard first. The head girl/lad will not be an available choice as she/he has to oversee the running of the yard in the employer's absence. The rider who shows the most promise as a potential competitor in their own right will not be a good choice either, for he/she will have aspirations to become a main rider for a professional yard. The best choice will be the groom that always turns up on time, takes care in his or her own appearance as well as that of the yard, is helpful and cheerful with a sense of humour, and who is above all a truly dedicated person working for a genuine love of horses. In fact, a groom that has all of the qualities of a *professional's professional*.

If the employer cannot find what he is looking for in his own yard, he is sure to look elsewhere rather than make do with the best of a bad lot. Some grooms may be thoroughly adequate at home, but show signs of strain when they have so much responsibility thrust upon them. It is an enormous responsibility and you must be able to cope with extreme pressure. All of your reactions have to be double quick, but through it all you must enjoy it or you will never stay the distance.

If you are hoping to become a travelling groom you should already have a good few years experience with horses. You must know how to cope with well-behaved or difficult horses in all situations, being able to handle them when they are excited or misbehaving. Either way, you must be able to control your temper.

You will find the job a lot easier if you are an unambitious competitor yourself. Indeed, if an employer realizes that you have competitive aspirations you will not be offered the job, as a travelling groom is expected to stay with the team on a long-term basis, getting to know how the horses and riders tick. It takes a long time to build up these relationships. However, once this has been achieved, you will become a big asset and an invaluable member of the team.

It is an advantage, but not necessary, to have an HGV (heavy goods vehicle) licence.

■ Different duties

You will not be at shows every day. On non-competing days your duties will be the same as any of the other grooms. You will still be expected to muck out and sweep up as usual. The travelling groom's position in the yard is not one of privilege. You are still a member of the working staff. On show days, however, you must come into your own, thinking for yourself and for the horses and riders. Strict attention to detail must be enforced, and nothing must be forgotten.

Although you will be an experienced general groom, competent in all aspects of horse management, you must also have a lot of common sense. Your greatest ambition should be to become an expert in boxing and travelling horses. A real damper can be put on the day if the horses are difficult to load for the return journey.

■ *Riders*

The riders for whom you prepare the horses may be your employers, be employed as riders, or may work alongside you in the yard being good enough to compete for different owners.

In a small competition yard the travelling groom will be expected to take care of both the horses' and the riders' needs at events. In bigger yards some of the travelling grooms will be responsible for the horses while the riders may have a personal groom (one that puts the riders' needs first, sharing pressures and responsibilities). A personal groom to a rider will be expected to know the exact requirements of that rider. For example, they will have to make sure that all of the rider's equipment, both for the rider and every horse that particular rider uses, is loaded on the box.

On arrival at the show you may be responsible for entering your rider in the right classes, getting the numbers from the secretary, or putting the numbers down at the collecting-ring. Other duties, such as cleaning boots and spurs, may also be your responsibility. You have to be at the rider's beck and call, not because they are lazy, but because they rely on you to take care of the tasks that they neither have the time for nor can be expected to worry about.

Throughout the day you must follow your riders' and the opposition's progress. You must always be at the ringside when they are competing. Should they have a fall or a mishap of any kind, you must be on the spot immediately to resolve the situation.

■ *Horses*

You may prefer to be responsible for the horses; they do not shout at you when you get something wrong! In this case, you may be allotted so many horses for the duration of the show. They may not be the horses that you are in charge of at home, nevertheless it is a good way of getting to know how to cope with all different sorts of horses. You will be responsible for packing all their equipment, such as tack, boots, studs, feeding equipment and grooming utensils.

Working with horses is more a way of life than a job – it would be foolish to pursue a career in the industry unless you have a real love for them.

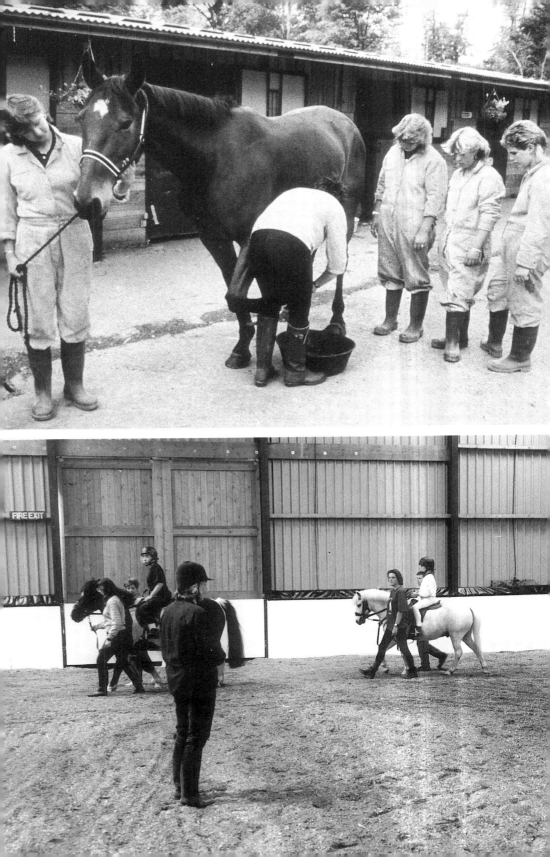

Your appearance plays an important role in finding employment. Here the rider is correctly and safely dressed for a riding assessment.

OPPOSITE

Above The learning process: Youth Training students at Bicton College being shown how to pick out a horses hoof correctly.
(P.J. Cook, Bicton College).

Below As a helper in a riding school, your duties will include leading beginner or nervous riders.

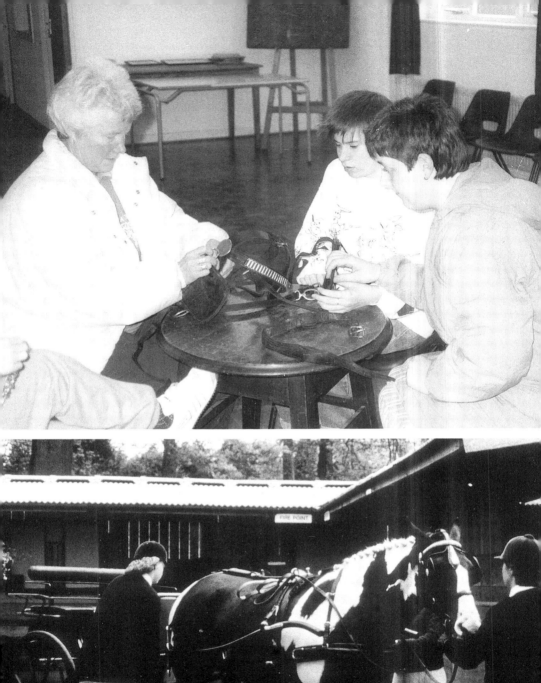
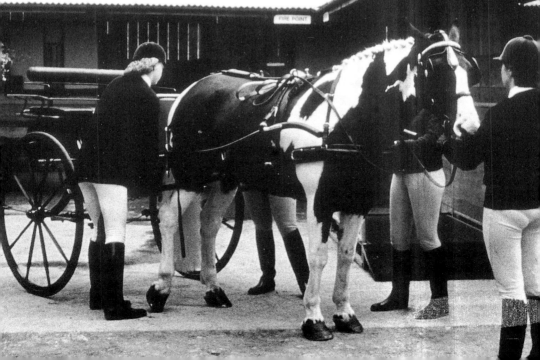

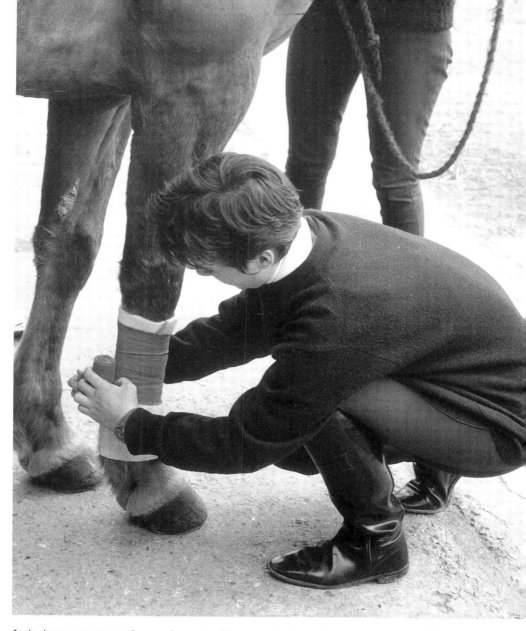

It is important to learn how to fit exercise bandages correctly. If the horse knocks himself in competition, he will not damage himself.

OPPOSITE
Above Learning how to clean, undo and put tack back together is essential for a position as a groom.

Below The end result – competent grooms adding the finishing touches to a very smart turn-out.

(*P.J. Cook, Bicton College*).

Many college-based equestrian courses offer the opportunity of learning computing and business skills – essential for anyone wanting to start their own enterprise.

OPPOSITE
A showjumping groom may be lucky enough to ride the novice horses in small competitions.

(P. J. Cook, Bicton College)

A travelling groom should know how to choose and fit all equipment needed for boxing. He or she should endeavour to become an expert in travelling horses.

OPPOSITE

Above There are good opportunities for enthusiastic grooms within the driving industry. Millie Millington, a very experienced whip and driving competitor, shows a less-able driver the ropes.
(Stuart Newsham)

Below The racing industry requires total commitment. A jockey's career is an extremely hard road to travel, but for those who succeed, it is very rewarding.

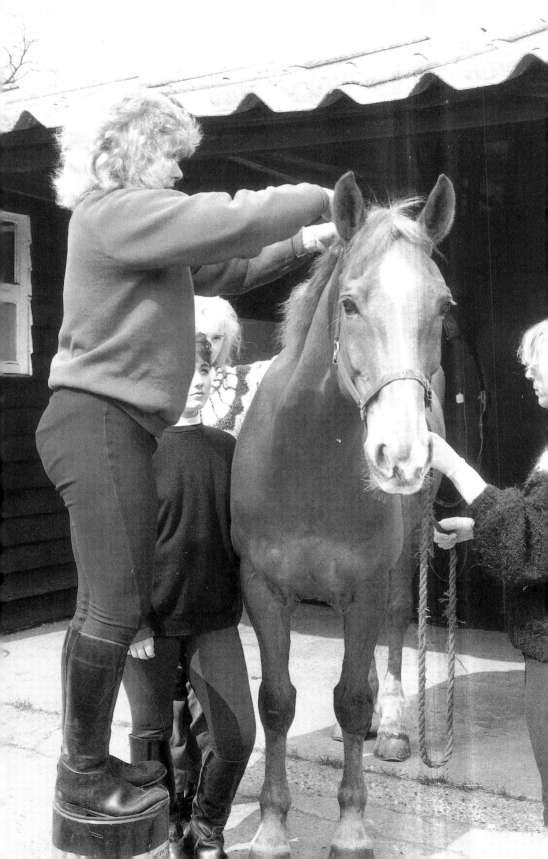

Mounted policemen and women have to undergo a meticulous and intensive training process, as do their mounts.
(Metropolitan Police, New Scotland Yard)

OPPOSITE
Preparing horses for shows involves plaiting up. Here students are learning how it is done.

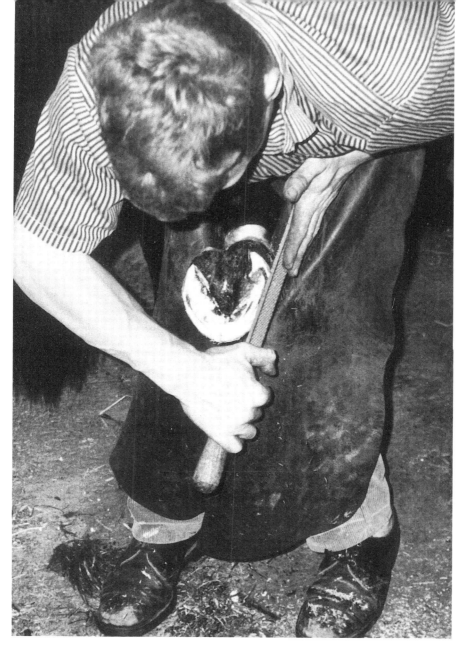

The farrier is a skilled craftsman and a vital member of the horse industry.

OPPOSITE
Above Experienced, knowledgeable grooms are hard to find and are often snapped up for more specialized work with horses, such as swimming handlers at hydro-exercise centres.

Below A career in the veterinary profession is one that needs dedication as it takes many years to train, and must be decided upon before taking A Levels at school.

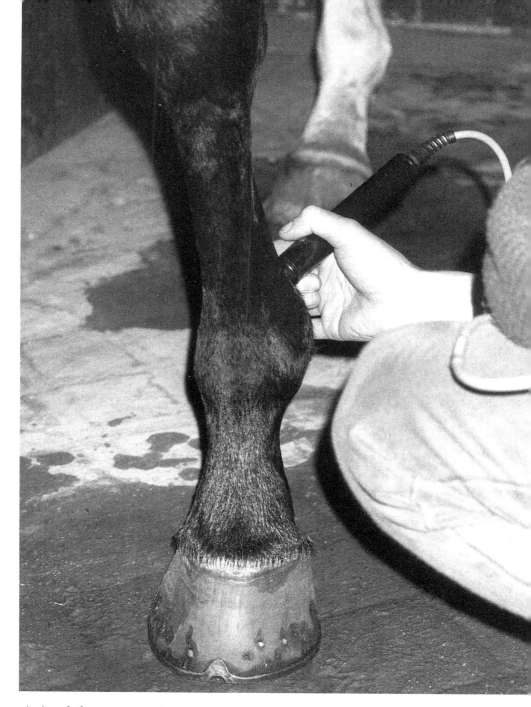

Animal therapy involves the use of lasers and is a specialized area of equestrian employment.

OPPOSITE
Only the highest standards of workmanship are acceptable in the saddlery trade.

(Cordwainers' Technical College)

Above Serving in a tack shop requires a good manner with customers.

Below The Riding for the Disabled Association provides the opportunity of riding or driving for people with disabilities, and there are plenty of ways of becoming involved.

The preparation of these horses for the show will probably be a joint effort from all of the grooms in the yard. However, once on the box, and indeed while loading, they will become your responsibility. You must ensure that they are loaded, and are travelled, as safely as possible. You may have to call upon all of your knowledge in loading young or difficult horses.

The horses with which you will be dealing may be worth an extremely large amount of money. You should not be overawed by this, but accept that your position is one that commands trust. A small cut that becomes infected through neglect may put a horse out for quite a while. This not only inconveniences the riders and upsets the owners, but also costs both of them money. At all times attention must be paid to every little detail. You should be the first person to notice a cut. You should be the first person to notice whether the horse is off colour, even if it is only slightly noticeable. No horse can perform its best if it is not 100 per cent fit and sound. Anything less than 100 per cent fitness can and will result in accidents.

You must come to know the mind of a horse. They cannot tell you how they feel, but through experience and years of handling different types, you will feel when they are trying to tell you something. Do not wait until it stares you in the face, it may be too late by then.

Bring anything that bothers you to the attention of your employer, whether you think it is trivial or not. Let him be the one to decide. Whichever course of action is then taken will be his responsibility. Do not try to shoulder all of the responsibilities of the team. This is not a groom's job or a travelling groom's job, but a manager's job.

RACING YARDS

The Jockey Club (see p. 123) has disciplinary control over professional horse racing, with the Levy Board in charge of finance. The day-to-day running and administration is carried out by the family firm of Weatherby (see p. 124).

While the Jockey Club issues the rules of racing, Weatherby's register every Thoroughbred horse foaled in Great Britain or Ireland, it records every horse and owner, and grades the horse for entry.

There are different types of racing within the sport as a whole:

Flat racing
National Hunt racing – Hurdle racing
National Hunt racing – Steeplechase racing
Point-to-pointing
Arab racing
Pony racing

Flat and steeplechase racing are the professional sides of the sport. The other categories are for amateurs only.

There are two options to think about when embarking on a career in the professional racing industry. The first option is to become a stable lad (this name applies to both male and female), working your way up to a managerial position. The second is to try to become a jockey. Although the starting-place for both is the same – at the bottom – there will be certain factors governing your suitability to become a jockey.

To become a stable lad you can either apply direct to a trainer, who will probably want you to have some experience, or you can apply in writing for a course to Major M. E. T. Griffiths, Director, British Racing School (see p. 123).

The aim of the British Racing School is to train stable staff for the racing industry. The school also offers opportunities for advanced courses aimed at potential jockeys and work riders. Their aim is to turn out 100 trained stable staff each year. If you happen to be the right size and show exceptional riding ability, you may eventually have the chance of becoming a jockey. If you succeed on a course with the British Racing School you will be offered to a suitable trainer.

If you seriously want to become a jockey, you must first of all be apprenticed between the ages of 16 and 24 to a trainer. At the age of 16, boys should weigh no more than 44.5 kg (7 st) and girls should weigh no more than 50 kg (8 st) if you are aiming to ride on the flat. You will at first have a lad showing you what to do; then, in normal practice you will be put in charge of two or three horses. You will be expected to take care of all their needs, including exercising and accompanying them to the races. At the training stables you will receive instruction, which will enable you if you are good enough to ride in races to see how you fare.

For those of you who are content to work as stable lads with the hope of promotion later on, it is advisable to find a position in areas of the country that are closely connected with racing. The greatest potential for employment can be sought from Thoroughbred stud work, stable work and work riding.

There is a minimum rate of pay, negotiated by the National Joint Council for Stable Staff, from the age of 19 years. Sixteen-year-old school-leavers can gain employment, but it should be understood that the pay will be proportionately less.

The National Trainers' Federation [see p. 123] helps boys and girls to find employment. The *Racing Post* and the *Sporting Life* also carry situations vacant in their classified columns.

Courses are also offered by the Northern Racing School in Doncaster. The courses are open to both sexes with a weight limit of 60 kg (9½ st). It is not essential to have any previous experience. Further details can be obtained from Mr J. Gale, Director, NRS (see p. 123).

If you are too heavy for the weight limits of flat racing, yet the racing scene draws you, there is a form of apprenticeship that has been introduced for *conditional jockeys* between the ages of 16 and 25. Although there is no formal training scheme for steeplechase jockeys, you will be given instruction by the trainer and if he/she feels that you are good enough, will consider letting you ride in races. Most conditional jockeys are ex-flat race apprentices who have become too heavy, although this is not a stipulation.

To compensate for the lack of experience, apprentices and conditional jockeys are given a weight allowance when competing, which they have to relinquish when they apply for a full jockey's licence.

Apprentice jockeys are still expected to 'do' their horses along with stable lads. Work begins very early in the morning, with a rest in the afternoon, then back to do evening stables. You will be dealing with highly-strung Thoroughbreds, so it is not a very good idea to pursue a racing career unless you have guts, dedication, patience and stamina.

It is a hard road to travel. The number of apprentices that make a success of a riding career is very small. However, do not let this put you off; just be aware of it and try harder. This, when succeeded at, is a most fulfilling career.

STUDS

Breeding is the foundation of all horse pursuits. Without the extensive work and dedication involved in all breeding establishments, commercial or otherwise, all competitive sports would grind to a halt. The need for experienced and trained staff is great.

The whole business of breeding is split into two different categories: Thoroughbred and non-Thoroughbred. Thoroughbred studs are mainly run as commercial enterprises, with the stock either being bred and prepared solely with the intention of racing in the breeder-owners colours, or sending them to be auctioned at the yearling sales. Thousands of pounds can be won or lost on the result of one horse. Stud fees for Thoroughbred racing stallions can range from under £1,000 to £100,000s, depending on the class of horse.

Grooms hoping to find positions in a professional Thoroughbred stud have to be very experienced, quick-minded and knowledgeable. People in the industry do not usually have the time to train people for the job, so it is certainly an advantage to have passed the NPS exams (see p. 72) or to have studied at one of the colleges that offers courses for the Thoroughbred industry (see Chapter 8).

There is also the Thoroughbred Breeder's Association (TBA), who will offer advice to anyone wishing to pursue a career in the bloodstock industry. They recommend that anyone hoping to gain employment should attend a course, and will supply literature on courses available for the Thoroughbred industry throughout the country. They will also issue potential stud workers with a list of TBA members willing to employ students, and help them by trying to place them either on studs or in bloodstock agencies.

Breeding within the non-Thoroughbred industry is just as hard a task, with everyone striving to produce the best horse for the job. There are studs dedicated to breeding pure horses of their chosen breed, such as Arabs, Welsh, Hanovarians, Irish Draught, Shires and pioneers of true English blood such as the Cleveland Bay horses. Each breed has its own society, and stock, both full- and part-bred, can be registered with each society and shown in breed classes respectively.

Alternatively, there are studs devoted to breeding competition horses from whichever mix of blood they care to try. It is popular to breed from non-Thoroughbred stallions such as Cleveland Bay or Irish Draught out of Thoroughbred mares to produce competition horses. The aim is to produce a horse of good conformation, with plenty of scope and ability, yet one that is a good straight mover with presence.

The National Light Horse Breeding Society has its own register of premium Thoroughbred stallions, aiming to give mare owners a good chance of breeding either show or competition horses, usually from part-bred mares.

Many horses produced in this way go on to become top-class horses in all different competitive spheres.

Employers in non-Thoroughbred establishments will usually take the time to train and encourage new workers. They run their stud and work as hard as they do mostly for their own satisfaction rather than hoping to earn vast sums of money, and as such are usually more tolerant of people wishing to join their industry.

SHOWING

The shop-window for the breeding industry is the show-ring. Although one cannot hope to make any money out of showing stock, it does provide an opportunity to show off the sort of horse a stud can produce.

Grooms who wish to find a job in the showing world should be of a calm, unflappable nature, with much patience. Preparing horses for the show-ring, whether they be ridden or in-hand horses, takes an exceptionally long time. Everything has to be just right. The task is made harder when dealing with young horses as they move about and fidget. The old campaigners of the show-ring, although they too have their moments, are generally easier to cope with.

Some of the jobs, such as trimming and plaiting, are tedious, and this is where your patience will be tried. The more irritable and angry you become, the worse the horse will respond.

There are many different categories in showing, some being solely for a certain breed: Welsh ponies, Arabs or Cleveland Bays, either ridden or in hand. Others are for a certain type: hunters, hacks, cobs or show ponies; young horses up to 4 are led in hand, horses of 4 and over are usually ridden.

You will have to learn how to stand, lead and trot a horse up correctly. You may or may not be able to show the horses yourself initially, but you may find it useful for the future. If you are asked to trot a horse up for the vet, for example, he will expect you to do it properly, so that he can make a correct diagnosis.

Many established people in the show-ring have a horse in each class at county level. One of your jobs, therefore, will be to have each horse ready outside the ring as the previous class ends, so that your rider can make a quick change. If the horses that are being shown from your yard are ridden horses, you may be required to warm them up if you are a good enough rider.

HUNTING

Grooms or Hunt Servants, as you will be known in hunting circles, must be prepared to work very hard. You may be expected to do a variety of jobs, which will include work with horses, hounds and people.

Generally, the staff are very well looked after. Many married couples are employed in the hunt service and may enjoy the benefit of independent accommodation.

Anyone wishing to make hunting a way of life, for that is what is required, must be able to accept a crowd of people who have their own way of doing things. They have their own principles and values, and acceptance of these without trying to change them will ensure a happy time.

Your duties will include exercising horses on the roads. You will probably need to be able to ride and lead, although hunt horses are generally older and more experienced, so you should not encounter too many problems. You will also be expected to prepare horses for travelling, bring home the first horses used and make them comfortable, then prepare for the return of the second lot.

Many hunting days do not end until very late, with most packs hunting approximately 3 days a week. Therefore it is not a job for the un-dedicated.

However, there are quieter periods when horses are turned away for the summer, although some attend parades of hounds at the agricultural shows. The summer is usually a time of preparation, when the younger horses may be brought on.

You will be working for a Master of Foxhounds, who usually has many years experience under his/her belt. Once an established groom you may be allowed by the Master of Foxhounds to carry out hound exercise and whipping-in duties. Men are mostly employed for the sole kennel-work as this involves the slaughter of horses and other animals as feed for the hounds. Within the larger stables there will be positions for huntsmen, kennelmen, whippers-in, exercisers and grooms.

DRIVING

There are good opportunities for enthusiastic grooms, especially if they have passed the British Driving Society's (BDS) Proficiency Tests 1 and 2. Placements can be quite varied, including positions for: combined driving trials (FEI); trotting horses; commercial yards/job master; coaching (private four-in-hand driving); show grooms; heavy horses; driving for the disabled.

If you wish to become involved in the world of driving it is a good idea to become a member of the BDS, as this will enable you to take the proficiency tests, which will show potential employers your credibility as a driving groom.

There is a Junior Whip section for anyone under the age of 18. The junior whips are well catered for. They have a much respected and admired commissioner, Mrs Caroline Dale-Leech. Not only is Mrs Dale-Leech an examiner for the BDS qualifications, but she also always tries to find positions for qualified Junior Whips or BDS members.

It is possible to train for some of the exams within the YT system (pp. 64–9), and you should be able to gain Tests 1 and 2. For other exams, courses are run by approved driving yards. For example, the Preliminary Groom's Test (p. 74) would take an average of 6 weeks, depending on your own ability. The Bicton College of Agriculture also has a driving option to its 'National Certificate in the Management of Horses' course, incorporating the BDS Groom and Carriage Driving Examinations (p. 73).

The training given for the driving exams is transferable to all areas of equestrianism, as all stable management is based on the BHS Stages (p. 74).

Your duties, once employed as a driving groom, may be quite varied, ranging from normal stable duties, harnessing up horses or preparing them for the show-ring. There is a great art in preparing the popular heavy horses for the agricultural shows that their owners so religiously attend. There are many old boys who have been doing it all of their lives, who spend most of their time on their big gentle giants. When you see the finished result you can understand why. When you have mastered the art of polishing the harness and harnessing up, preparing all different types of horses for driving, both in the ring and at work, and perhaps being a competent driver yourself, you will find no difficulty in acquiring a position which commands respect and rewards your work.

TREKKING

Trekking centres do a lot of business in the summer months, catering for the holiday trade. As such there are opportunities for either part- or full-time employment. The advantage of working in a trekking centre is that you will be coming in to contact with all sorts of people. Young, old, good or novice riders, all are after one thing: a pleasant few hours spent roaming around the countryside on horseback. However, this does not make your job any easier. Indeed, you have to be alert all the time, as you are responsible for people of all ages and abilities from the time they get on to their mount to the time they get off.

3
Running your own business

So far we have looked at careers where you will become an employee of an equestrian establishment. You will probably be very happy working within such an environment. However, there are other possibilities you may wish to consider should the opportunity occur.

When you have gathered much knowledge in the ways of the equestrian world and have many years experience, you could try to build up a yard of your own. There are very few who have made a fortune from such enterprises; it is enough to try and make the enterprise pay without trying to make huge profits. The reasons for wishing to work for yourself must come from a deep longing to be your own boss, run your own yard and truly feel that you have that something extra to offer both human and equine participants in such a venture.

If you do have the urge to have a go, you should decide what skills you have to offer and in what part of the industry they will be welcomed.

WHAT CAN YOU OFFER POTENTIAL CLIENTS?

The first thing you should do is to sit down and work out what you have to offer potential customers. Although what you are hoping to achieve is to run your own horse establishment successfully, you must look upon it foremost as a business. Without this aim, you, as many before you, will fail. No matter how good you are, your business will not survive unless it pays for itself. Nobody will help you unless they can see that it has the potential to be a viable money-earning proposition.

The best approach is to start out small and hope to expand when the time is right. In this way, you can hope to keep your head above water, but if the worst should happen you will not have incurred too many debts.

Other than the basic upkeep and management of horses, the bare essentials to think about in each enterprise are listed in the following examples.

THE BREEDING INDUSTRY

You could try to run a small breeding enterprise, being responsible for the care of broodmares, foals and youngstock. The more adventurous, or those with more help and experience at the beginning, may wish to try and stand a stallion.

On the commercial side of the industry are the Thoroughbred breeding establishments. Those who are well aware of the requirements of Thoroughbred breeding will try to breed either for the yearling sales or stock to sell or race, as appropriate. Many other breeding establishments breed part-breeds, Arabs, ponies, natives or other pure breeds either for sale or competition.

Special knowledge required:

(a)   Care of broodmares at all stages
(b)   Foaling – care and attention
(c)   Weaning – when and how
(d)   Training of youngstock
(e)   Showing – breaking-in
(f)   Marketing stock

If the stud hopes to stand a stallion:

(a)   Stallion management
(b)   Covering of mares

Requirements:

(a)   Plentiful grazing
(b)   Safe, secure fencing
(c)   Foaling boxes
(d)   Excellent veterinary advice

Expenses (other than general upkeep)

(a)   Veterinary expenses
(b)   Stud fees (including keep charges)

COMPETITION YARD

You will need to be either an accomplished rider or a knowledgeable trainer in your chosen sphere before starting such a venture. It also helps a great deal if your name is well connected within the specialized area in which you wish to teach.

Special knowledge required:

(a)   Experience of training and schooling young horses.
(b)   Experience of re-training problem horses.
(c)   Experience of training young, novice or advanced competitors.
(d)   Knowledge of all sorts of tack and how to fit and use it.
(e)   Course building.
(f)   Being aware of all competitions available in your chosen discipline.
(g)   Experience of buying and selling.

Requirements:

(a)   School – indoor or all weather.
(b)   Training equipment, jumps, etc.
(c)   Range of different horses.
(d)   Yard and paddocks.
(e)   Horsebox.

Expenses (other than general upkeep):

(a)   Competition fees
(b)   Horsebox expenses
(c)   Training equipment
(d)   Travelling expenses

RIDING SCHOOL/LIVERY YARD

These two are put in the same category as they can be successfully combined. You will have to be a qualified instructor, or employ one. The better qualified the instructor, the more the yard has to offer. For example: a BHSAI will attract beginners and pleasure riders, whereas a person who has a BHSI or Fellowship will attract serious career students, competitors and/or owners wishing to have their horses trained. Therefore, in theory at least, the better the qualification, the better the business.

Special knowledge required:

(a) The working routines of riding schools.

(b) Being able to deal with people.

(c) Experience of instructing riders of all abilities.

(d) Money management.

(e) Being responsible for the public and the horses.

Requirements:

(a) A range of different horses, for novice up to advanced standard

(b) School

(c) Good hacking

(d) Parking facilities

(e) Experienced instructor/s

(f) Licence

Expenses (other than general upkeep):

(a) Purchase of good school horses

(b) Wear and tear

(c) Constant farriery

(d) Equipment: tack, hard hats, etc

RACING YARDS

The racing industry is a very professional world. Only those who have made it as jockeys, or those who are related to and/or have trained with established trainers, or who have exceptional experience and knowledge within the racing world, have a chance. To persuade owners to let you train their horses, you need a good reputation. To get a good reputation as a trainer you need to have owners who are willing to let you train their horses. It is a vicious circle where only the best survive.

One way of trying to make a start within the racing world is to train and run your own horses. It will cost you a great deal. However, if you get some good results you may build from there, with owners offering you their horses.

WHERE TO START

Once you have decided what type of establishment you want to set up, you need to arrange the finances. However, before you can do this one or two more important decisions must be made. To start up a yard you will need to find premises. You do not have to go out and find a ready-made yard, however. A place that needs renovating and modernizing, or a field with planning permission for a yard, are good examples of a starting point from which you can build up a business.

A few places come up on the market for sale. If they are sold with the 'good will', that is, a business that still has customers wanting the service offered, or an ongoing concern, this could be an option for you to consider if it should come your way. However, you must avoid at all costs a yard that has a bad reputation. Although you can change the name and advertise the fact that it is under new management, bad impressions last. Unless you intend to offer a different service or to expand and change the whole outlook of the place, it will be safer to look elsewhere.

Some of you may be lucky enough to have parents who own farms or have land with their houses. This is an ideal situation from which to build, as you could probably cut down some of your overheads at the start. Although in this situation you will not have to purchase a property or a lease, you should not expect to have the use of the land and/or buildings free. If you are running a business with this sort of aid from your family or friends, they are entitled either to be paid rent or to make a stake in the profits when the yard is established.

FINANCES

You should at this stage be fully aware of how much money you are going to need to get you started. This includes premises, animals and all other initial expenses.

You may or may not be aware of where the money is going to come from. One thing is certain – unless you are very wealthy in your own right, you will need help. If they are able to, your parents may be willing to help you initially, either in the form of a loan or as partners in the business.

While you were still employed as a groom, you should have made acquaintances. These are the people who could help you to get started. It may be that they thought enough of your ability as a rider to allow you to school their young horses, either for competition or to sell on. Even if they do not have horses themselves, they will recommend you to other people if you have made a good enough impression. Remember, personal recommendations carry a lot of weight.

Perhaps you do not feel that this is the right way for you to start. In this case a more formal approach to starting a business would be to apply for a loan at your bank. A local business adviser at your bank would be a good person to have a talk with. They may help you financially to start up a business if they can see that you have a good idea, are very determined and prepared to work hard for what you want. As well as helping you, they are looking at your business as an investment. The better you do, the better their chance of conducting your financial affairs in the future.

Once you have secured the initial costs, you will want to look for ways of securing your future. At the start you should make at least enough to cover your expenses and a small wage for yourself. It can take up to 2 years for your financial position to stabilize. Only then can you tell whether or not it is working.

SPONSORS

Many established competitors look for a sponsor to help with expenses.

There are many people involved in equestrian sport who are looking for sponsors. You must, therefore, present yourself as the best choice for them. Your proposal must be arranged in a business-like way. It is advisable to spend considerable time in putting together a document about your career. You should include all of your achievements to date and your aims for the future. Any photocopies of press cuttings or photographs of you in action are well worth including.

When approaching a potential sponsor, you must inform him of what he can expect for his money. You must be realistic when doing this, he will not want to be disappointed. The following are points you could offer:

– Horses competing in the sponsor's name and colours.
– Horsebox carrying sponsor's name and possibly colours.
– Rider wearing items carrying sponsor's name and colours when not competing (the British Equestrian Federation at Stoneleigh should be advised if you intend to do this.)
– Rider conducting press interviews.
– Rider attending a number of company functions for the sponsor.

It is worth remembering that the lucrative sponsorships sometimes achieved by top riders have been won by many years of proving themselves. They probably started out with a small sum, which is what you are hoping for. In the beginning, you should think in terms of leasing one or more horses for one or more years. The sponsorship, subject to the agreement of your owners, should finance the cost of keep, training, travel and competition expenses for each horse.

Your best chances may come from companies either with strong local connections or in related industries. You should be able to provide a reasonable assessment of costs per horse. The sponsor will then have a fair idea of whether or not he is prepared or able to help you.

OTHER WAYS OF RAISING FUNDS

Once your yard is running to a normal routine, you could introduce other activities. As well as making extra money, you could give a lot of pleasure to young children by running courses and events for children on holiday. Apart from the usual horse management courses, where they will improve their horse knowledge and riding ability, you could include fun activities. Adventures such as treasure hunts, day-trips to horse shows or even yard water fights, not only make the course a success for both you and the children, but they will also make the children and their friends want to return every year.

Another source of income, if you have enough grazing, is to take racehorses out of training. Many horses are boarded out to quiet yards where they will be turned away for a good few weeks, or even months, at the end of the flat or National Hunt season. Many of the racing yards do not have much in the way of grazing facilities, therefore they have to send their horses away for a holiday. Many horses who have had this type of holiday start the next season as fresh as their first. You will of course have to ensure that you have the necessary experience to deal with racehorses and that you take all the required safety precautions, including insurance.

Within a riding-school or livery-yard environment you could combine a service for hunter, competing or schooling liveries. Hunter liveries are boarded on a full-livery basis, whereby you will be responsible for their daily exercise and grooming as well as their normal requirements. Other than this, you will be expected to prepare and maybe travel the horse to hunt meetings. Hunter liveries pay well, and a few regular customers will bring in a steady income.

Competing and schooling liveries are slightly different as, once you have done your job, the ride or even the horse may be taken from you. Some people only wish to have their horse schooled on for them to compete when it is more experienced. It could be that you will not be required to school the horse yourself, but to train the horse and rider together. An association such as this with horse and rider can be very rewarding. As well as seeing the combination improving, you can also take pride in their hoped-for success. However each of the competing liveries is to be trained, the income that you will receive from them will fluctuate as horses are taken away or brought to you throughout the year.

Another avenue of business is to take horses in solely to prepare and travel to events. Young show horses are often kept in this way, and return to their breeder or trainer only at the end of the show season. The one problem with this type of custom is the time involved. As said before, it takes a long time to prepare horses for the show-ring. Many horses may be young and therefore need extra time and gentle handling. Unless you have plenty of time or know somebody who enjoys doing the job and will work for you on the required days, you should give this option a great deal of thought before embarking on it.

4

Other alternatives

If working with horses as a rider, groom or instructor does not appeal to you or does not suit your circumstances, but you still want your work to be connected with horses, there are other options. Some of these might particularly suit a person who wants to concentrate on competing on their own horse on an amateur basis, or who has horses of their own to look after.

SECRETARIAL WORK WITHIN HORSE ORGANIZATIONS

Many employers within horse organizations are looking for office workers who not only have secretarial knowledge but experience with horses as well. They are looking for people who know the horse jargon, so that they can relate easily to people within the equestrian world.

If you think you might be interested in this line of work but do not have secretarial experience, you could do a full-time or evening course. Alternatively, you could apply to the company concerned, enquiring whether they are prepared to train people as secretaries who are knowledgeable within the horse scene, such as yourself.

There are many organizations which employ such workers. Companies involved directly with the everyday management of horses or companies within related industries all need secretarial staff. Some small organizations such as feed merchants, riding clubs or charities are likely to need this type of secretary just as much as large organizations such as the British Horse Society, Weatherby's or the British Show Jumping Association.

Many positions of this type are advertised in the horse press. You could apply to companies enquiring whether they are thinking of employing new secretaries within the near future. Other jobs involving secretarial skills might be found within transportation or bloodstock agencies. The latter also employ people interested in research and investigative work into Thoroughbred blood lines, as do horse auctioneers.

EQUESTRIAN WRITING AND JOURNALISM

Writing or reporting for magazines or newspapers is a very competitive field. As well as taking in everything you hear or see and then being able to relate it as you heard or saw it, you must also have a flair for writing.

A career in journalism can follow on from a secretary's position. For example, a secretary to an editor of an equestrian magazine may be given the chance of covering a few local shows or point-to-points. If their coverage is good, a journalist's career may be born. In order to make writing interesting and accurate, the writer must be involved within the equestrian scene. You are a person who has been involved and you could be the person an employer is looking for.

You could of course apply for jobs advertised, or send an example of your writing to magazines and papers enquiring about a reporter's position. You must be able to show that you are well equipped with knowledge of the local show scene and that your work makes interesting reading.

Alternatively, you may wish to try and write articles for publication in magazines. If you can show that you know a subject extremely well, you may be considered for writing a weekly column. You will also double your chances if you are able to supply photographs to illustrate the pieces you write. For information on training for a career in journalism contact the National Council for the Training of Journalists, tel: (0378) 72395.

PUBLIC RELATIONS

Public relations, although a relatively new field within the equestrian industry, is experiencing great growth. It offers many opportunities to someone with plenty of drive, ambition and flair.

If you are thinking of trying to become employed in this area you will have to know your subject, for you will be required to deal with business people and companies who expect good results.

PR is an extremely important part of business marketing. You will need to be able to develop sound promotional concepts, following them through every stage of their development. The ability to write well about your clients, generating editorial exposure, is the most important aspect, for yours is the job of letting the public know who your clients are and what they do. Being creative and thinking up *new* ideas is also valuable, as these will grab the public's attention more readily than the usual worn-out ones; however, you must be realistic.

Trying to get a job in PR is not easy. You will need to push yourself hard, taking a junior position with a good public relations company at first, then working your way up. Many people wishing to join the industry are graduates, but that is not essential, especially if you are confident in discussing equestrian matters.

A job in PR can lead to many exciting opportunities within the equine industry; from working with many others in a large company with important equestrian-related clients, to working on your own for a top showjumper who wants to keep in the public eye. The openings are there if you look hard enough, and as long as you can write accurately, giving your editorial that little bit of sparkle, and be diplomatic when dealing with clients, you should find the job very worthwhile.

FARRIERY

Farriery is a very skilled ancient craft dating as far back as the Roman Empire.

Care of horses' feet is necessary whatever purpose the horse is used for; even broodmares and youngstock that are not shod regularly need their feet trimmed and shaped. Therefore, the farrier is not only a necessity for working horses, but a vital member of the horse industry.

The farrier is a skilled craftsman who has much knowledge and experience. Knowing how to make, fit and remove shoes to good feet, as well as how to prevent and correct bad feet, comes from years of practice in the trade. However, these are not the only requirements of a good farrier; as well as knowing how to treat horses' feet, he must also know why he treats them as he does, being able to explain the theory behind the practice.

The first step when considering a career in farriery is to find an approved training farrier who will take you on as an apprentice. An approved farrier is one who is in Part One or Part Two of the Register of Farriers and is also entered on the list of Approved Training Farriers.

There are a few requirements to be met before an apprenticeship can be considered. You should be between 16 and 25 years of age. If you are older than this you will still be considered, but will not be eligible for a grant. You must have GCSE grade E or higher, or equivalent, in English and Mathematics.

Once you have found a training farrier, you will have up to, but no more than, a 12-week trial period when your time will be spent constructively, gaining relevant practical experience. If you show a genuine aptitude for farriery, at the end of the trial period you should submit a joint application for apprenticeship, with a signed certificate from your approved trainer, stating that you have been in satisfactory service with him for not more than 12 weeks.

Once your application has been assessed and you have been accepted by the Registrar of the Farriers' Registration Council, you will be invited for an interview and to take practical and written tests at the School of Farriery, Herefordshire Technical College. If you are successful you will be able to embark upon a 4-year apprenticeship, for which an apprenticeship agreement must be signed. The first 3 months of the apprenticeship will be a probationary period.

At the beginning of the apprenticeship you will be supplied with a copy of the farriers' code of conduct, which you should bear in mind at all times during your training and the following years. Your training will be carried out with your training farrier, combined with short periods of residential training taken at the School of Farriery. At the end of 4 years, which signifies the end of your apprenticeship, you are required to take the Diploma of the Worshipful Company of Farriers (DipWCF).

Once you have successfully completed your apprenticeship and passed the DipWCF you will be a qualified farrier. However, it does not finish there. A qualified farrier must register, on completion of the apprenticeship and passing the DipWCF, with the Farriers' Registration Council. All persons shoeing horses are required by the Farriers' Registration Act 1975 and 1977 to be registered annually.

Farriers, after completing their apprenticeship, passing the DipWCF and registering can, if they so wish, seek higher qualifications. The Associate of the Worshipful Company of Farriers (AWCF) carries the accolade of the highest technical merit and can be taken 2 years after passing the DipWCF. The Fellow of the Worshipful Company of Farriers (FWCF), which requires a farrier to be able to lecture on the subject, can be taken not less than 12 months after obtaining the AWCF and 5 years after passing the DipWCF. A candidate is required to submit a thesis for this examination.

If you are interested in a career in farriery, you can obtain more information from either:

The Registrar, Farriers' Registration Council (see p. 122); or The Registrar, National Joint Apprenticeship Council, Avenue R, 7th Street, N.A.C., Stoneleigh, Kenilworth, Warwickshire CU8 2LS.

SADDLERY

Saddlery is also an old-established craft. The existence of a guild of saddlers can be traced back to the late twelfth century.

Today, after many hundred years, the Worshipful Company of Saddlers continues, among other fundamental principles, to encourage the highest standards of workmanship in the saddlery trade.

The traditional method of starting out on a saddlers' career is to approach a master saddler and ask him/her to take you on as an apprentice and to train you. If you do not know of any saddlers in your area, you should contact the Chief Executive of the Society of Master Saddlers:

Mr H. C. Knight, The Cottage, 4 Chapel Place, Mary Street, Bovey Tracey, Devon TQ13 9JA.

If he does not know of a saddler to approach at once, he can supply you with a booklet containing master saddlers' names and addresses.

Once you have begun your training, you may be sent by your employer for a course at the Rural Development Commission in Salisbury. Training is only arranged for people who are already in the trade. It is very difficult to find a member of the Society of Master Saddlers who will take you on. It is a very skilled and dedicated job, and it takes many years to learn the skills required. If you are determined enough and are prepared to live away from home so that you can be near or at your place of work you may find a willing, patient employer.

If you are not successful in your search there are alternatives. At present there are a few organizations running training courses. Certain entry requirements and the content and length of courses may vary. Each course will, however, have the necessary facilities and be able to assess your abilities at different levels of skill, which will enable you to achieve qualifications recognized by the trade. You can apply to the following for information:

1. The Cordwainers' Technical College, Mare Street, Hackney, London E8 3RE.
2. Walsall Leather Training Centre, 56/57 Wisemore, Walsall, West Midlands WS2 8EQ.
3. Cambridge & District Saddlery Courses, Pinfold End Farm House, Pinfold End, Hawstead, Bury St Edmunds, Suffolk IP29 5NU.

As it is difficult for apprentices to find a willing trainer, various forms of training, such as the courses run by the preceding organizations, have been developed in recent years.

There are recognized standards required for the saddlery trade. The levels of skill are specified at four levels as follows:

Level I   General basic skill in the use of materials and tools, and the manufacture of simple items of saddlery under supervision.

Level II   Specific skills in one of the following: saddlemaking, bridlemaking or harnessmaking, with limited supervision.

Level III Specific skills in two of the following, to a satisfactory standard without supervision: saddlemaking, bridlemaking or harnessmaking.

Level IV Skills at Master Saddler Level in saddlemaking, bridlemaking and harnessmaking to the standards required for licentiateship of the City & Guild Institute. This requires the ability to specify tools and supervize the work of others, together with mastery of a range of relevant knowledge and skills, and the ability to apply them.

Your first step is to apply for saddlery skill assessments on the appropriate form to The Chief Executive, The Society of Master Saddlers (see p. 53). You will then be advised of the extent of the assessment for which you have applied, and the likely dates of the next examination and the centre to which you have been allotted.

For more information and queries apply to The Clerk, The Worshipful Company of Saddlers (see p. 124).

The Cordwainers' Technical College provides two full-time courses with saddlery content: The College Diploma in Leathercraft & Saddlery is the course they recommend to those intending to set up their own leathercraft/saddlery workshop. The one-year certificate in rural saddlery course prepares students for the City and Guilds Certificate in Rural Saddlery. This is structured as a series of 10-week modular components that will allow you to acquire training in stages, perhaps on a block-release basis, for those already in employment (see p. 78).

Local education authority grants are normally available for students wishing to enrol on these courses. Entry qualifications are flexible, but they are basically the same as BTEC National Diploma levels (see p. 98).

MOUNTED POLICE

The mounted police are today fulfilling a tradition of service that goes back to the eighteenth century. Their history began in 1760 when Sir John Fielding, the Bow Street magistrate, developed a plan for mounted patrols to deal with the plague of highwaymen infesting the metropolitan area's turnpikes. In 1836 they were incorporated into Sir Robert Peel's newly established Metropolitan Police.

There are only a few mounted branches attached to the forty-three separate forces in England and Wales. These are naturally in large cities such as London, Manchester, Liverpool, Birmingham and Leeds. Entry to any specialized branch of the police is by selection from the regular strength. This means that there is no direct entry. Even if you have an aptitude for and commitment to working with horses, you will have to join as an ordinary constable and then seek a transfer after 2 years probationary service, as and when a vacancy arises.

Any officer wanting to join a mounted branch must show a good grounding in general police work first. It is most important that you be the right type of person; someone with a personality and temperament that fits into a small, close-knit team, therefore only one out of five applicants is accepted into the Branch.

You will need to be under 76 kg (12 st) in weight to be considered, although you need not have any experience of working with horses, because once you get past the preliminary interview stage this would be remedied during an intensive, 22-week initial training course. You will live at Imber Court, the Branch's Central Training Establishment, learning riding and stable management and basic veterinary care of your mounts. The mounts are changed every month to give you maximum experience with a number of different horses.

A normal term of duty for the 200 horses and most of the 239 officers that make up the Mounted Branch consists of a 3-hour patrol followed by care and maintenance of mounts and their tack.

The main tasks are general traffic control, street crime, rowdyism, autocrime and theft, but where the Mounted Branch excels is in crowd control. This can vary widely from ceremonial occasions, to football matches, to demonstrations – and even riots. It is estimated that a trained officer on a trained horse can be as effective as a dozen foot officers in such situations.

For more information you should contact the Directorate of Public· Affairs, Metropolitan Police (see p. 122).

VETERINARY NURSING

The Veterinary Nursing Scheme, for the recruitment, training and registration of veterinary nurses or animal nursing auxiliaries as they were known before 1984, was introduced by the Council of the Royal College of Veterinary Surgeons (RCVS) in 1961.

A veterinary nurse's job is to assist veterinary surgeons in their work. Although the scope of the work involved can be quite varied, it is illegal for a veterinary nurse to carry out any form of veterinary medicine or surgery. Both before and after qualification, their duties are to assist in carrying out veterinary work only under the direct supervision of a veterinarian. Nevertheless, the work involved entails considerable responsibility. It is well recognized that veterinary nurses carry out their nursing duties competently, quickly and with the least amount of explanation needed from veterinary surgeons.

The veterinary nurses' profession is a relatively new one. However, they continue to be well respected by the veterinary surgeons and public alike. A veterinary nurse is expected to maintain the highest standards of nursing care and conduct at all times.

To train as a veterinary nurse you must first find gainful employment, of not less than 35 hours per week, at an approved training centre. Approved training centres, with a few exceptions, are veterinary practices which have been recognized by the Royal College for this purpose. Once you have found such employment you can apply for enrolment as a trainee veterinary nurse. The work that you will be expected to do is essentially practical in nature, therefore most of your 2-year training is given on the job in supervised day-to-day work. The theoretical background knowledge that is necessary may be obtained partly from your place of work and partly from attending a part-time course given at your local college of further education. It is possible to carry out part of your training at certain agricultural colleges. Full-time residential courses are either offered as instruction over one or two terms as part of the 2-year training period or as a series of 1- or 2-week courses spread over 2 years.

It is advisable to arrange a trial period before trainee enrolment, so that you can make quite sure that you have the necessary aptitude and ability to work as a veterinary nurse. Once you are satisfied that you want to pursue a career in veterinary nursing, you can formally apply to the RCVS for trainee enrolment. There are certain requirements that have to be met before an application can be made under the scheme. These are:

i   Passes in four different subjects at grades A, B, or C at GCSE level or their equivalent, which should include a pass in English Language and a pass in either a physical or biological science or in mathematics.
ii You must be 17 years of age or over.
iii You must have the consent of your parents or guardian if you are under 18.
iv You must be gainfully employed at an approved training centre or have the promise in writing of such employment.

Before you can become a qualified veterinary nurse, you must pass two examinations set by the Royal College of Veterinary Surgeons: the Preliminary Examination, followed by the Final Examination. Once you have completed your 2-year training period (which does not have to be continuous) and passed the examinations required, you will be eligible for entry on the List of Veterinary Nurses. On qualification, you should have adequate knowledge and be sufficiently adaptable to undertake a wide variety of tasks.

VETERINARY SURGEONS

A career as a veterinary surgeon is one which should be decided upon before embarking upon your A-level course at school. There are few opportunities at university to switch to a veterinary course from another course. Although a number of mature students are considered for courses each year, they must be able to fulfil all the requirements of the university of their choice, as with any prospective candidate. Even then, no one can be certain of a place, as the number of applicants far exceeds the number of places available.

The requirements for admission to one of the six universities in the UK offering courses leading to degrees in veterinary science, veterinary medicine or veterinary medicine and surgery, are normally five passes in approved subjects at GCSE and Advanced level, at least two of which must be at Advanced level. However, those are minimum requirements and candidates should aim for three A levels in appropriate subjects with at least two at grade A.

To obtain a veterinary degree you will have to undergo a long, arduous course of education. Firstly, you will have to spend a trial period with a veterinary surgeon to establish for yourself the genuineness of your ambition. Further study and training at university would normally extend over 5 years, or 6 years at the University of Cambridge, before graduating with a veterinary degree.

So, as you can see, it is extremely difficult to become a veterinary surgeon and as well has having the academic requirements, regard and concern for animals is essential.

Veterinary surgeons on qualification, and admission to membership of the Royal College (signified by the letters MRCVS after their names), must promise that their constant endeavour will be to ensure the welfare of animals entrusted to their care.

If you are still at school and are seriously considering a career as a veterinary surgeon, you should write to the university of your choice to obtain a copy of the prospectus for the veterinary degree course and ask for any advice that you might require.

Further information about veterinary nurses or veterinary surgeons can be obtained from The Royal College of Veterinary Surgeons (see p. 122).

ANIMAL THERAPY

Anyone wishing to work as an animal physiotherapist must first train and qualify as a chartered physiotherapist in the human field. This will then be followed by a minimum of 2 years postgraduate experience working with humans, usually within the National Health Service.

After this period a chartered therapist may become a pupil with a veterinary practice or animal physiotherapists. They remain a pupil until two veterinary surgeons are prepared to certify that they have successfully transferred their skills from humans to animals. Eventually, this part of the training will be replaced by a validated course in animal therapy – again, only open to those qualified in the human field.

As with the veterinary profession, you must decide on this type of career early on in your final school years. This early planning will give you the advantage of taking the right examination for your proposed career. The entry requirements to train as a chartered physiotherapist are the same as for either the veterinary profession or any degree or diploma course. A minimum of five GCSEs and two Advanced levels. The GCSE subjects should include passes in English and at least two science subjects, the A Levels should include a biological science.

There are other routes into physiotherapy. For example, a BTEC National Diploma in Science (Level III) or a science Higher National Diploma may be considered. There are specialist schools of physiotherapy, usually attached to hospitals, where students may train. However, almost half of the students train at universities or polytechnics.

As we are talking in terms of 7 years plus before you can undertake the specialist work of treating horses, you will need to be a special kind of person. Apart from the academic requirements you will need to be a good communicator, tolerant, patient and caring. You will need a sense of humour and to be reasonably fit.

The specific interest group involved with animal welfare is the Association of Chartered Physiotherapists in Animal Therapy.

For more information about approved courses you should contact the Chartered Society of Physiotherapy (see p. 124).

SALES-PERSON

Anybody can sell horse food! This might be the opinion of an outsider to the industry. The importance of feeding horses correctly is well known, and everyone should appreciate the knowledge required to understand why they should be fed one foodstuff rather than another. A good feed sales-person will not only advise you what to feed your horse on, they will also tell you *why* to feed it. Put yourself in a feed merchant's shoes. If you can explain to people why they should feed certain food, it not only makes you a good sales-person, it also makes them happy customers.

There are other requirements as well as a knowledge of horse foods. You should have a good, natural business sense. You will be required to add up quickly, work tills and write receipts, as well as having a friendly personality for dealing with the public. You may not think that the latter is important, but people often come in to shops as much to have a chat as to buy horse feed.

Many people are setting up their own animal food sales businesses at their own yards and livery stables. It is convenient for them to have somebody who can work in the shop and help out in the yard at quiet times. In this sort of position you will obviously need to be versatile.

If you have your own place with barns, you may well have thought of the idea yourself. As well as the trade that comes into the shop, you could run a delivery service. Many feed merchants also sell other horse goods, such as tack and riding gear. It is very convenient for the public to shop at one place, so if you can build up a good stock of many different items, both popular and obscure, you will soon be doing a good trade. Your reputation will be built up by word of mouth and it does not take long to get around. If you can keep a constant line of stock, people will come to you with the confidence that you will have what they want or can get it for them quickly.

To work in tack shops you also need to know the subject. If a person comes in to buy a certain item, you need to know what it is they are talking about before you can help them. Not everybody comes into a shop and picks something off the shelf. Many want to see what you have, and you should be in a position to advise them why they should buy it. Although you should never push anything on customers, some people do need prompting to buy things. This is where you will have to learn to be a good sales-person. To know when to give advice or when to be quiet is the name of the game.

There are many other jobs for sales-people and representatives within the horse world. Many involve travelling around. Positions such as insurance representatives, feed representatives or representatives for veterinary medicines all require you to travel and deal with the public.

With these types of jobs there may be certain perks to be gained. You will probably get a company car as you could not do your job without one. You may be able to buy goods at discount prices, or you may get plenty of free samples.

Some jobs will require you to work for commission. You will be paid a percentage on every thing you sell, whether it be feed or insurance. The more you sell, the better you do. If you turn out not to be a very good sales-person you will not earn very much. Until you have learnt the trade, therefore, you are probably better with a salaried position. Once you know that you can sell products well, you can make up your own mind.

RIDING FOR THE DISABLED

Of all the ways in which horses are used the best of all is for giving pleasure to people with mental or physical disabilities. It takes a special type of person to give their voluntary help to Riding for the Disabled. If you feel that you can help, all you need do is contact your local branch or write to Riding for the Disabled Association (see p. 121).

If you feel that you would like to do something to help, but could not work with handicapped people, there are many other worthwhile jobs such as fundraising, help with secretarial work or even being willing to help at social functions, where you would be most welcome. Any little help that you can give, in whatever capacity, will give handicapped people the opportunity to enjoy the sport of kings, the sport that many of us take for granted.

The Association is a nationally registered charity. It gives training to enthusiastic, dedicated and willing helpers, at local, regional and national level. The Association has many recurring needs, these are: suitable horses and ponies; voluntary helpers; special equipment for riders; training of instructors, therapists and helpers; conference facilities; covered riding schools; sponsorship for publications and films and transportation.

While trying to build your own career, it would be nice if you could try to give help, in some way, to provide the opportunity of riding to disabled people, who might benefit in their general health and well-being.

TRAINING AND QUALIFICATIONS

5

Training schemes for school-leavers

In this day and age the best advice must surely be to get yourself qualified. Hopefully you will have started thinking about a career with horses young enough to have been able to acquire a certain degree of competence in the skills required of an equestrian employee. Maybe you will have taken advantage of the opportunities described in Chapter 1.

You may gain theoretical knowledge from books and reading, but there cannot be any substitute for practical experience. You will not know how you will react in certain situations until they occur.

If you can prove yourself to be proficient in the skills required for a groom, you may get an employer to take you on straight from leaving school, although you will of course need further training. If you have had no dealings with the horse industry before, or are of very limited ability, you should consider getting yourself better qualified and further trained.

Your two basic choices for gaining full-time employment are: to leave school with the hope of finding employment straight away, or to move into higher education, getting yourself some sort of recognized qualifications (see Chapter 8).

EMPLOYMENT STRAIGHT FROM SCHOOL

Should you decide to leave school at 16 and seek employment, you need either good academic qualifications, or a basic degree of knowledge in horse management with the ability to show potential employers what you know and understand. Employers have a whole host of trained and qualified people applying for jobs, and you have to prove that you are a worthwhile candidate. You may only get a short interview, so be truthful, but show that you are efficient in the work that you are capable of, and are willing to learn.

You should start applying for jobs before you leave school (see Chapter 6). It can take some time from the first application to the position of actually getting the job. Apply for all of the jobs open to you for which you have the necessary qualifications and experience. Every job will have plenty of applicants. You must apply early by post or telephone as required. At the interview you will be asked relevant questions about the work that you will be expected to do. A shrewd person will be able to tell from your answers whether or not you will be able to apply yourself successfully to practical situations. You have only one chance at each interview, use it well.

Always remember that you are wanting a worthwhile career, so do not jump at the first job offered regardless of its worth to your future. If, for instance, you are offered a job without a proper interview and are told to start tomorrow, just stop to think why? Why would a person be in such a position as to be without staff, and unable to get any? Why can't they keep staff? There are occasions, of course, when through sudden illness or bereavement, employers are left needing staff urgently. The reason for the urgency to start and the lack of staff will become apparent once you visit the place of work; then you can judge for yourself. Just be careful.

■ *Work experience from schools*

This is a scheme run by many schools. You will be allowed to go to a place of work for a certain length of time, being excused from school. This will usually be for a week or maybe two, although it might take the form of one day a week for a certain number of weeks. It is hoped that by doing this you might see whether the job, or at least the type of work, suits you.

If your school does not have a policy for such schemes, you could try talking to your careers teacher or headmaster/mistress. In your last year at school you will probably have meetings with your careers teacher from time to time. You should discuss the matter with him/her at this time. You will find that he/she is very helpful in guiding you towards a job which should suit you. Make it clear if you intend to leave school at 16. You may stand a better chance of being allowed to do work experience. Discuss where you would like to go and ask your careers teacher if he/she can try to arrange it for you to go to a place of your choice or somewhere similar.

If you are very keen to go to a particular place to carry out your work experience, try motivating yourself. Enquire whether the yard or business will take you on. If they agree, then approach your careers teacher for permission.

GOVERNMENT TRAINING SCHEMES

There is at present Youth Training, whereby you can leave school and start training in a designated yard or work place. Usually you will have your accommodation found, and receive a set weekly allowance. You are encouraged to train towards equestrian examinations, such as those of the British Horse Society (BHS), the Association of British Riding Schools (ABRS) and the National Pony Society (NPS). Such exams fit easily into the pattern of National Vocational Qualifications. The training for these exams is also an integral part of most college courses and training schemes.

Various training schemes have been introduced by the government to provide structured foundation training, administered by the Training Agency of the Department of Employment through Training and Enterprise Councils. Apart from the work experience and training you will receive, you may also be required to attend a college or similar centre either one day a week or on a block-release basis.

For information on the availability of places in your area, you should contact your local Careers Service Office, Job Centre or your local Department of Employment office.

Let us look at organizations that apply to general equestrian employees wishing to work in all spheres, rather than a specific area.

The examinations set out in the table are designed so that you can train as you work, and normally follow the day-to-day running of training establishments.

The Scottish Trekking & Riding Association and the Pony Trekking & Riding Society of Wales also have qualifications available: Grade III, II, and I Instructor's Certificate.

Apart from racing, most opportunities for anyone wishing to start a career in the horse industry will be provided by the government training schemes. These have become the recognized route of entry into employment and/or training and take various forms from time to time according to government directives. Try to make sure, when taking up a position on one of these schemes, that you will be given

Examinations that can be taken during a two-year Youth Training scheme

Organization	YT Level 1	YT Level 2	YT Level 3
BHS	HK & C Stage I HK & R Stage I	HK & C Stage II HK & R Stage II	HK & C Stage III HK & R Stage III + Preliminary teaching test = BHSAI*
ABRS	Preliminary horse care & riding certificate Level I	Preliminary horse care & riding certificate Level II	Assistant Groom's certificate
NPS	Stud Trainee's certificate		Stud Assistant's certificate
EEB	Phase I	Phase II	National Certificate in the management of horses

* Subject to the academic requirement of four GCSEs
Note: In exceptional cases a trainee with appropriate experience may progress beyond the levels shown above.

BHS   British Horse Society
ABRS   Association of British Riding Schools
NPS   National Pony Society
EEB   Educational Examining Bodies

the opportunity and encouragement to take the relevant examinations for the part of the industry in which you wish to work. Ensure that you join a scheme using the Industry Preferred Training Pattern (IPTP).

The syllabi for exams run by the BHS, ABRS and NPS at this level include: stable routine; grooming and general care of the stabled horse; watering and feeding; management; saddlery; horse clothing; shoeing; veterinary; riding; lungeing; administration and safety codes.

Details of the examinations you should be encouraged to take while on one of these schemes follow.

■ *The BHS and Youth Training (within the overall BHS examination system)*

The minimum age of entry for the BHS Horse Knowlege and Care (HK & C) or Horse Knowledge and Riding (HK & R) Stages is 16. You must start at Stage I and work upwards. The HK & C section and riding section may be taken as separate tests leading up to the full Stable Manager's Examination and the Fellowship of the BHS (FBHS). In this way, those who have no desire to ride still have a course open to them that tests their knowledge in stable management, with a recognized qualification at the end of their study.

For Stage I you will be required to understand the basic principles of working with well-mannered grass-kept and stable-kept horses, under supervision. For the riding section you will also be required to manage a quiet and experienced horse in an enclosed space.

Before entering Stage II you must have passed the BHS Riding & Road Safety Test. You must understand the general management and requirements of horses for their health and well being, and be able to lunge. You will still be under regular but not constant supervision. For the riding section you will be required to manage a quiet horse in the countryside and on the public highways, as well as in a ménage.

The minimum age of entry for Stage III is 17 years. You must be able to show the ability to look after four horses, stabled and at grass. Your riding ability should be more varied, in that you will be expected to ride a variety of horses in many different situations. A written test will also be included.

Even if you are just taking the HK & C section, you should still be a competent enough rider to be able to take horses on ride and lead exercises.

Stage IV may only be taken when you reach the age of 18 (20 from 1 January, 1993), so this could follow on after your YT course when you have progressed sufficiently.

You will be required to take sole charge of a group of various horses of various types, both at grass and stabled. You must be capable of training and improving horses in their work on the flat and over fences.

If under 18, you can take your BHSAI (Assistant Instructor) exam only if you have the academic requirement of four GCSEs grade C or above. This is achieved by passing the HK & R Stage III exam and the

Preliminary Teaching Test. If you have sufficient GCSEs you can enter at 17½. You will be examined in your ability to give instruction in basic subjects.

You may enter the Preliminary Teaching Test when you have passed the HK & R Stage II. However, you will only be awarded the BHSAI when you have passed both the PTT and HK & R Stage III. This is the minimum qualification that must be held by a person licensed to run a riding establishment under the Riding Establishments Acts 1964 and 1970.

At the time of application for all exams you must be a member of the BHS.

Any queries regarding BHS examinations should be made in writing to the British Horse Society, enclosing a stamped addressed envelope. They will also be able to provide you with a full approved training schools list. Choose the centre best suited to your needs and apply to them direct (see the directory of training centres in Chapter 7).

■ *ABRS and Youth Training*

The ABRS make excellent provision for young people wishing to start a career with horses. They strongly encourage 'helpers' to attend riding schools, and to follow through with courses and exams for every stage of training up to the Riding School Principal's Diploma.

They advise that although previous government training schemes would perhaps not give you the intensive training that courses structured for examinations might, they are now coming into line and will give you a good base from which to start, plus an opportunity to reach a certain examination or NVQ level (see p. 75).

The ABRS Preliminary Horse Care & Riding Certificate Levels I and II are open to those who are 16 or over and who are in work training with horses.

To take the Preliminary Horse Care & Riding Certificate, you must have completed the requirements of the syllabus during your training/work period. The certificate is designed to be a guide for employers as to whether you are fundamentally employable.

Level I   You should be able to show the basic ability to carry out simple routine tasks.

Level II   You should have the ability to carry out most common tasks, and some understanding of any task carried out.

The exam is entirely of a practical nature. The tasks required have to be performed correctly, efficiently and safely.

You will be required to know the areas as specified in the syllabus to a good standard, capable of being learnt within the 2-year period. Level I candidates will not be required to jump or lunge as Level II candidates are.

Apply to the Secretary of the ABRS for an application form and details of the fees for your exam. Having received your completed form the Secretary will forward to you confirmation of an examination placement. Other examination syllabi are also available – again apply to the Secretary enclosing a stamped addressed envelope.

■ *NPS and Youth Training*

The National Pony Society also runs a youth training scheme designed to meet the needs of 16- and 17-year-old school leavers, with emphasis on breeding and stud work.

It is intended that this 2-year scheme will become the normal route of entry into the industry. The NPS has approximately 100 placements in England. Trainees receive a weekly allowance and an accommodation allowance (where applicable).

The aim of the Youth Training that the NPS provides is to prepare young people for a working life in the horse industry through a foundation of planned work experience and vocational training.

The duration of the scheme for 16-year-old school-leavers is based upon 104 weeks. This is to include a minimum of 20 weeks (100 days of 6 hours) off-the-job training and further education, 36 days holiday plus 16 Bank and public holidays. The normal working week over the period of the scheme is 40 hours with a 5 or 6 day working week. The scheme will last for 2 years.

The duration of the scheme for 17-year-old school-leavers is of 1 year's duration (52 weeks) with a minimum of 7 weeks off-the-job training. The aim of the scheme is to provide competence in a job and/or a range of occupational skills. You will be encouraged in your first year to achieve:

i   NVQ Levels 1 and 2 in Horse Care and Management.
ii NPS Stud Assistants' Certificate Parts 1 and 2;
    and in your second year:
i   NVQ Level 3 in Horse Care and Management.
ii NPS Stud Assistants' Certificate Part 3.

When you embark upon your training you will register for the appropriate National Vocational Qualification. When you do so you will receive an NROVA (National Record of Vocational Achievement) (see p. 76). As your training progresses your achievements are assessed and recorded. When you have completed each particular level you will receive a certificate which should be kept with your NROVA.

WORKING PUPILS

The traditional method of training is as a working pupil in a riding establishment. The normal rules for the working pupil scheme are that the pupil works at the yard in return for tuition, although terms vary from place to place. Some establishments provide accommo-dation, meals and pocket money, but it is not unknown for a working pupil to be required to pay for board and lodgings. There is no set age at which you may become a working pupil, as in the YT scheme.

Although there are many large, recognized establishments that take working pupils, it is not compulsory that they provide training. You may find that a small yard run by qualified staff will suit you better. However, be sure, if you choose this option, that the yard has all the necessary facilities for training you properly.

When you consider you have sufficient knowledge to take the exam that you are working towards, you will have to apply to sit the exam at an approved training centre near you. Apply to the organiz-ation/society whose exam syllabus you have been following and they will advise you how best to go about it.

The successful working pupil is conscientious, enthusiastic and has a real desire to learn.

■ *The BHS recommended working pupil outline contract*
It is recommended that the following list of points should be covered in a working pupil contract and agreed by the riding school/stable proprietor and working pupil before the course commences:

1 A broad description of the duties that the working pupil will be expected to carry out.
2 Hours of work.
3 Time off, to include weekends.
4 Arrangements for public holidays.
5 Other holidays.

6 The training that the pupil will receive, both mounted and dismounted.

7 The examination for which the working pupil will be trained and the approximate date of the examination.

8 Who will make the entry for the examination.

9 Accommodation to include bedding and linen, etc.

10 Provision of meals.

11 Keep of working pupil's horse, if any.

12 Taking part in competitions, if any.

13 Hunting, if any.

14 Practical teaching experience.

15 All financial arrangements.

16 Period of probation.

17 Any rules of discipline with regard to the pupil's conduct, e.g., dress, hair-styles, make-up, time-keeping. etc.

RECOGNISED QUALIFICATIONS

An outline of further qualifications obtainable from the different organizations follows. This should give you an idea of what to aim for eventually (see also the 'Career Paths' chart, p. 10). There are exams at all levels from school age up to mature adults. There are minimum, but no maximum age limits, for certain exams, and most are progressive.

■ *BHS examination system*

The BHS exams are not aimed specifically at the stud or racing industry. Their courses are designed more towards those wishing to make careers as grooms, competitors, yard managers, trainers or instructors and are recognized world wide. The number of candidates taking these professional exams has risen annually and now exceeds 11,500 a year. The table shows the traditional examinations available.

Apply to the Executive Officer, Training, Examinations and Approved Riding Establishments, at the BHS offices, for more details, or a syllabus for each exam.

■ *ABRS examination system*

The ABRS is the professional examining body for grooms in the UK and provides an excellent examination system catering for the whole industry.

The ladder of progression through traditional BHS examinations

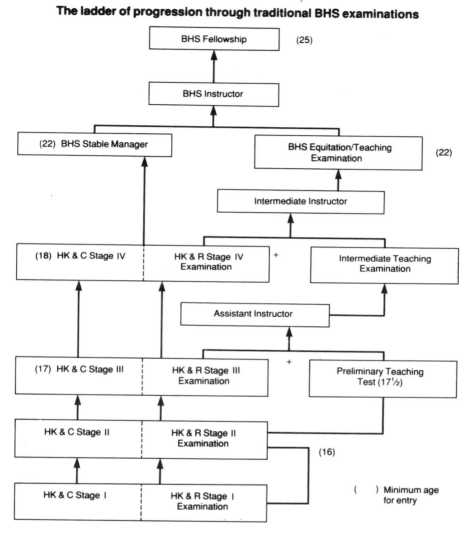

The ABRS have a really refreshing approach to the whole business of exams and qualifications. Nobody is too small, too young or too old, to take a test to better themselves. They aim to provide nationally recognized standards of competence at whatever level you feel happy with.

The ABRS has a career and examination structure that is not only programmed to fill an employment need, but to help raise the standard of horse care and management generally.

As well as the Weekly Riders Tests and the Preliminary Horse Care and Riding Certificates for Youth Training, Levels I and II, there are other examinations available for career-minded students.

The ABRS Assistant Groom's Certificate

You must have had 1 full year's experience (full-time) and be 17 years and 6 months old before the examination is open to you. It is intended to show employers that you are a competent groom, being able to work on your own yet still requiring some supervision.

The ABRS Groom's Diploma

You must have had 2 full years experience (full-time), and be 18 years and 6 months old, before this examination is open to you. It is also a requirement to have already passed the Assistant Groom's Certificate and to hold a current first aid certificate.

'Honours' are awarded for candidates who attain exceptionally high standards of competence. It is intended to show employers that you are a competent groom, capable of working on your own and organizing the work of other staff if required. No GCSEs are required for these examinations.

Further qualifications that may be obtained after many years of experience are:

The ABRS Riding School Principal's Diploma.
The ABRS Riding Master's Diploma.

A syllabus for each of these exams can be obtained from the ABRS Office. Enclose an sae.

■ *NPS examination system*

The two main examinations that can be taken with the NPS are the Stud Assistant's Examination and the Diploma Examination.

The Stud Assistant's Examination can be taken in three parts. Each part may be taken separately. The first two parts may be taken at any time after the commencement of the course, but the third and final part may only be taken after 1 year's training and candidates must be 17 years or over. The examinations are held at a number of centres throughout the year from April until October. To prepare for these examinations it is necessary that you train at an NPS-approved stud.

Having passed this examination you will be a competent worker in the horse industry, doing your work with thought, care and efficiency. You will, however, still need some managerial supervision and guidance.

The Diploma will become available for you to take only after you have passed the Stud Assistant's Examination and gained a further 3 years experience. The Diploma is a professional qualification, being Level Four (see p. 74) in the levels of horse care and management.

Having passed this qualification you will be competent as a stud groom, being able to manage all of the stud duties correctly. You will also be capable of being left safely and efficiently in charge of a stud.

You need not have any academic qualifications to train for these examinations, or any prior experience when starting to train for the Stud Assistant's Examination.

■ *The British Driving Society (BDS) Proficiency Test system*

The British Driving Society, being the parent body for all driving enthusiasts in Britain, aims to encourage and assist everyone interested in the driving of horses and ponies.

The society has proficiency tests in four grades, as shown below, to enable members to confirm their driving ability. The Groom's Test leads to a joint BDS City & Guilds Carriage Driving Groom's Diploma – a professional qualification. The examinations are approved by the Joint National Horse Education and Training Council.

The junior drivers or 'whips', as drivers are called, are well catered for. They have their own commissioner, and are offered two annual scholarships for driving tuition at a leading establishment.

The now well-established Proficiency Tests are organized by the BDS Test and Training Committee and are completely voluntary.

Test 1 Preliminary

For single-horse driving only, to a simple but safe standard, to include a basic knowledge of harness, vehicle care and suitable horse management, including minor ailments.

Test 2 Intermediate

As Test 1 but to a more advanced level of knowledge and understanding and a higher practical ability. Candidates may take an optional extra section for pairs driving.

Test 3 Advanced

A test of a very high standard. Very correct turn-out and driving technique is required, as well as a good sound theoretical knowledge of harness-work and a good understanding of horse care and management. There is an optional extra section for pairs and tandem driving.

Groom's Test

Only a preliminary standard of driving is required for this test but the knowledge of turn-out, harness theory and stable management is to a very high standard. Those holding British Horse Society, Riding Club or Pony Club qualifications to the equivalent standards will be exempt from the stable management section of this test. This test can lead to a professional qualification for carriage grooms with a City and Guilds/British Driving Society Diploma.

Preliminary Groom's Test

This test is designed to be achievable by YT students or trainee carriage-driving grooms. It requires a basic understanding of horse knowledge and care to Levels One and Two (see below) and a basic understanding of working with the preparation of harness horses.

With the exception of the Groom's Test, only BDS members are eligible to take Proficiency Tests 1, 2 and 3. A certificate will be issued to all successful candidates.

Anyone wishing to take these tests should apply for the syllabus and application form. For more information contact the secretary at: The British Driving Society (see p. 120).

THE CHANGING FACE OF EXAMINATIONS AND TRAINING

In 1987 the Joint National Horse Education and Training Council (JNHETC) was formed. It is responsible for all aspects of training and education in the horse industry.

The JNHETC produces the Levels of Horse Care and Management books 1 and 2, which are guidelines to acceptable standards at each level of training within the indusry. These levels are defined as follows:

Level One (basic)	Has the ability to carry out simple routine tasks.
Level Two	Has the ability to perform most common tasks plus an understanding of any task carried out.
Level Three (competent workers)	Proficient within the skills listed and a competent worker in the horse industry.
Level Four	An experienced worker with particular competence in the specialist knowledge and skills shown.

Level Five | A person who exhibits the competence, knowledge and skills to supervize/manage a skill.

Level Six | A person with the skill and knowledge to teach and ride to an advanced level, to lead within the horse industry and to represent the industry.

The JNHETC is working in conjunction with the National Council for Vocational Qualifications (NCVQ) towards the acceptance of a recognized national framework for skill assessment and qualifications within the horse industry.

NATIONAL VOCATIONAL QUALIFICATIONS

National Vocational Qualifications (NVQs) are being introduced in all industries. The qualifications are designed to fit into a simple framework, clearly showing which career routes will be open to you. The system of qualifications is easily accessible to anyone working or training within the industry.

Organizations that already offer professional examinations may award NVQs as and when appropriate to those who achieve competence in their work. It is hoped that there will definitely be four NVQ Levels and possibly a fifth one for those wishing to earn 'professional status' within their own area of the industry.

Each qualification will cover an area of work, so that employers will know that someone who has an NVQ at a certain level is qualified to do the work required in that area, at the level of qualification achieved. The framework of qualifications will also make clear to the employee the paths of progression to higher levels and any opportunities for transfer to other areas of work.

The qualifications themselves are made up of separate units that can be assessed and recorded separately. For the basic qualifications at Levels 1 and 2, you will be required to reach a standard of competence in a range of core units covering:

- Health and safety at work with horses
- Basic handling of horses
- Watering and feeding stabled horses
- Stable routine
- Grooming and care of stabled horses

- Basic care of horses at grass
- Horse clothing
- Saddlery/harness
- Horse health
- Transporting the horse
- Care of the horse's foot
- Lungeing/longreining

with other options taken into account:

- Equitation
- The racing industry
- Heavy-horse work
- Breeding

Each unit is divided up into elements, and competence must be shown in each element before you can successfully achieve a full unit. You need to do this for all units at each level before you will be awarded an NVQ at that level.

You can enter for all of the units required for an award at one time, or enter for a few at a time, building up 'credits' towards certification at your own pace. Your achieved units will be collected and kept in the National Record of Vocational Achievements (NROVA), this being the national system for credit accumulation for NVQs. Once you have successfully achieved the compulsory core units you will be awarded the Horse Industry's Level Certificate at the level in which you have succeeded.

Certificates are awarded for competent performance in work activities. Where possible the competence of employees is assessed in the work-place, opening up the qualifications to individuals who cannot take time off for traditional training. You will be awarded these qualifications as long as you can show competence in your work performance; your age, where and how you became competent or how long it took you are all irrelevant.

Your knowledge will be assessed by means of a standardized multiple-choice question paper or by question-and-answer conducted during a practical assessment. This assessment will take the form of observation, questioning essential knowledge and, where circumstances require, questioning about procedures. Such questioning will be directly related to the practical task in hand.

Your 'assessors' may be college staff, riding school instructors or senior members of staff of other equestrian establishments.

6
Further education and training

If you want to continue in education after leaving school, you have to decide whether you want to concentrate on equine studies – horse knowledge, stable management, instructing and so on – or whether you want to combine them with other courses. You may want to study for more GCSEs or A-Levels, or to do a secretarial or business studies course as well, depending on what type of job you eventually want. If you definitely want to work with horses, as a groom or instructor, you may want to go straight into employment, looking for a job that allows you to study part-time on a day-release or block-release basis. For those who want professional qualifications in order to pursue a particular career in a particular field, such as the Thoroughbred industry, specialist courses are available.

You might want to attend a technical or agricultural/horticultural college in the hope that you will get a better position once you join the industry. You may choose to go to a college that incorporates riding, stable management or teaching exams, perhaps working towards being a qualified instructor.

Throughout the United Kingdom there is a growing number of horse study courses, and the choice of course can be a difficult one. Make a list of all the points that are important to you, for example:

learning to ride	learning to teach	close to home
stud work	Thoroughbred industry	competition work
length of course	part- or full-time	accommodation
saddlery	farriery	training methods
breaking and schooling	lungeing	other studies
social activities	finances	end results
agricultural studies	technical studies	horticultural studies

Request prospectuses from the colleges that offer courses in the areas you are interested in. If you can, find out about the colleges from someone who has a working knowledge of them. Match up your list of what is important with the aims of the colleges, their grading and entry requirements, and compare their facilities. Make a shortlist of the most suitable and apply to them for an interview.

At this stage you are not committed to anything, so try to apply yourself with an open mind and listen to what is being offered. Ask all the questions you want, for it is too late when you get home. It is a good idea to make a list of questions you want to ask before going, as they can soon slip out of your mind when somebody else is talking.

Chapter 8 details equestrian-based courses offered by a number of colleges around the UK. To help you make the right choice, you should seek sound advice from people whose job it is to know about prospects for different careers and career courses.

■ *Help from the Careers Office and officers*
The Local Education Authority maintains the Careers Office. It is there to offer you guidance and information on careers. It will also help people at school or college, or older people, with details of training, job seeking, and other opportunities. Most offices have a careers library, which includes leaflets and pamphlets for your benefit. You will also be able to make use of the careers officers; they are there to help and guide you should you require assistance. They are specially trained and can interpret the local scene.

DAY/BLOCK RELEASE FROM WORK

While release schemes from schools help you to decide whether or not a type of job is for you, release schemes from work help you to obtain more qualifications while still training.

■ *Day release*
You can take advantage of part-time study while still training in employment. Your employer may release you for half or one day a week to study for recognized qualifications at college.

■ *Block release*
Your employer may allow you to study at a college for recognized qualifications for continuous periods, usually several weeks long. This could be useful for short, intensive courses, where the employer should benefit from your extra knowledge.

WHERE TO LOOK FOR JOBS

■ *Local contacts*

You may have some of your own contacts already in the equestrian world. These people may be sufficiently involved in the equestrian world to know of a vacant position. If they do know of a job going, ask them if you may use their name as a reference when approaching an employer. The horse world works very much on the grapevine, so you may well hear of a job before it is advertised, enabling you to act quickly and get in first.

Make it known to your friends and contacts that you are looking for a job, asking them politely to bear you in mind should they hear of any in the future. A personal recommendation to an employer from one of your friends will do a lot to help your chances.

■ *Use your initiative*

As previously mentioned, you should have started applying for jobs before you leave school. Take the initiative by asking local stables and studs whether they are expecting to have a job going in the near future, in this way you may get first consideration should a job come up. You can also advertise the fact that you are looking for a job in your local post office, newsagents or local press for little cost. You might also put an advertisement on your local saddler's/feed merchant's board. Someone may pick this up; local employment is always an advantage for an employer as it reduces the need for accommodation.

■ *Employment agencies*

You have the option to enrol on an employment agency's register. You will be required to supply a comprehensive profile of yourself and of the work that you have accomplished to date. They in turn will circulate lists of potential employees to employers who have shown an interest. They will also send you details of immediate vacancies. Before enrolling you should find out exactly how their system works. There are many different agencies giving various degrees of satisfaction to both the workers and employers of the horse world. As ever be careful, making sure that you read all the small print.

Most agencies carry positions for a wide range of different jobs requiring different skills, including: instructors, grooms for hunting, livery, riding schools, polo, driving, showing, eventing and dressage. They will also introduce you to employers for head girl/lad, working pupil, riders' and trainees' positions for full- or part-time employment. You will find the addresses of these agencies in equestrian magazines.

■ *Newspapers*

Your local newspaper is a very good way of advertising your services. Many employers advertise in the local press for grooms. Scan the classified advertisements daily or weekly as applicable. As soon as you see a job advertised that suits you, enquire immediately by letter or telephone as requested. In the local newspapers the advertisements for horse work will probably be included in the 'Horse & Rider' section, as this is where the interested parties will be looking. Make sure if you are placing an advertisement yourself, that this is the section it will be included in. Adverts such as the ones illustrated are not uncommon in the local papers.

Situations Wanted

16-year-old school-leaver seeks employment to gain experience. Anything considered.
Tel._____ anytime.

Mike is 19, has his BHS Stage 3 and Preliminary Teaching. Wants to work in a dressage yard or a teaching position.
Tel: _____ after 6 or leave message on answerphone.

Situations Vacant

Trainee grooms required for racehorses. Must ride well and be willing to be trained to a high standard. Good wages and accommodation.
Tel: _____ for further details.

Working pupil required. Excellent opportunity for young person to join team at small, friendly BHS stables. 100 per cent pass rate BHSI examination. Excellent facilities. Small wage. Apply in writing including CV to: _____

■ *Equestrian press*

Equestrian magazines also have advertisements as above, the best for job vacancies being the *Horse and Hound*.

The job advertisements are split into different sections, usually Situations Vacant and Situations Wanted, although positions for hunt masters or joint masters will be found under the masterships section. The pupils/tuition section also includes places for those interested in working pupil places and further training. Many of the training establishments advertise in this section for career students.

A LOOK AT POTENTIAL EMPLOYERS

Horses, as you know, are a way of life. For those of us who think of little else, they are our passport to sanity.

Many people keep horses just for their own pleasure. The actual cost of keeping them may be more than they can really afford, but they manage. However, to embark on a career in this environment will not put you in good stead for the future. There will always be the fear that one day they will have to get rid of their horses, and you will be left out on a limb without any formal training. This type of situation might suit an older, more experienced person who likes a change from time to time. It will not do for a career-minded person who wishes to gain more experience and to train in a systematic way.

When embarking on a career, you must give serious thought to where you want to end up, as this will determine where you should start. If you want to work in the racing industry it is not much use to take a job in a riding school to tide you over, as this is not the type of experience you need or want. It will not impress an employer from a racing yard and it will not do your ego any good. Start the way you mean to carry on, even if it means putting yourself out. You may have to travel further than you wanted or wait a little while longer for the right position.

By maintaining your own standards an employer can see that you have seriously thought out where you want to be and what you want to be doing. And if you can put yourself on the right track, they may consider that you will be able to keep their horses there as well.

Knowing how to deal with an employer for the first few meetings can be tricky. It will help if you know what sort of discipline is enforced in the yard before you have a meeting. This will help you in knowing how to act and just how to answer the questions that you are asked. One employer may require you to be very strict with the horses, and usually this sort of person will be strict with you. Another may be quite laid-back with the horses, and in turn you. The more you can find out about a potential place of employment before you go, the more you will know about your potential employer before your interview.

Successful employers create a successful yard by keeping their employees' loyalty, respect and lasting service. It is therefore harder to find employment in such places, but hopefully your advance planning will have given you an advantage over the rest of the competition. A place in such a yard will help you to secure better jobs in the future.

A questionnaire sent to a range of employers produced some interesting results:

1 Most employers preferred replies to advertisements to be made in writing, although some said that they would prefer a phone call to fix a date for an interview.
2 Nearly all employ full-time staff, about two-thirds employ part-time staff as well. Only just over one-third were willing to take working pupils, while two-thirds were willing to take YT students.
3 Most would be prepared to take teenagers for work experience from schools, quite a few already doing so.
4 Just over half said that there was a chance of promotion, depending on age and ability, and over one-third said that they would consider it.
5 Surprisingly, only a very small number of employers said that they would allow pets. Of these, two accepted horses free of charge while others expected livery fees to be paid. One also said a dog or a cat would be acceptable.
6 Over three-quarters of employers preferred non-smokers, although some stated that this was not essential.
7 A driving license was considered an advantage, especially an HGV, although again this was not essential.
8 Just under half said that you must have previous experience, one-quarter stated that no experience was necessary, and about half of both these groups said that they were prepared to train the right sort of people.
9 Depending on the position applied for, most said that official exams, such as GCSEs or BHS exams were an advantage, but not necessarily needed.
10 The preferred age for employees was 18-21, although this heavily depended on experience.

11 Most employers preferred single applicants, due mainly to convenience.

12 Most didn't mind either sex, there were some preferences for females (due to the accommodation arrangements), but not one reply stated a preference for males.

13 Most had accommodation available if required, some requiring you to live in as family.

14 Only a few said other duties were required; these included housework, general farm work and gardening.

15 A lot had chances for grooms to compete and travel, depending on ability, if they wished to do so.

16 Interviewees were preferred to dress practically but smartly, bringing riding wear if applicable.

17 Most provided insurance cover and had a good policy for days off. Usually 1 day a week and 2 weeks a year for permanent staff.

Here are some of the comments from employers who answered the questionnaire. The question was: What advice would you give to a potential employee wishing to work in your yard?

Employer 1   Good manners are essential. An ability to carry out instructions – to be flexible and to show enthusiasm. An ounce of keenness is worth a library of qualifications. Pride in one's work – to 'look the part' at all times.

Employer 2   Advice would really depend on the age and experience of the employee. I look for an honest, hard-working person with commitment. They must be caring, eager to learn and receptive to criticism. Above all, the welfare of their charges (the horses) must come first. However, I am nevertheless a caring employer!

Employer 3   Above all they must have a willingness to pay attention to detail, enjoy the work and work towards an exam if possible. Be cheerful, reliable and ask questions. Don't be afraid to discuss problems. Be punctual and tidy. We always like to see that young people have at least tried to work at school, and gained some exams, particularly English. They must also realize that it costs time and money to train them correctly, and should not be looking for high wages at 17 – rather a good, thorough training.

Employer 4   They must be pleasant, friendly, hard-working, honest, neat and enthusiastic.

Employer 5   Spend a week with us and see if you fit in. We are only interested in people wishing to work to a high standard.

Employer 6   Punctuality. Discretion. High standards.

Employer 7   Depending on the position applied for:
1. Work hard, watch carefully, learn and don't be frightened to ask.
2. Go to someone immediately with a problem of any kind. Initially the head girl/stable manager, then the boss.

Employer 8   Do your work well, enjoy the work that you do. Discuss all problems before they really become troublesome.

APPLYING FOR JOBS

Now that we know a little more of what employers expect in general, we can get down to the business of applying successfully.

Let us consider replying to advertisements by letter. Unless you have very neat handwriting, you should try to type a letter or ask someone to do it for you. When applying for anything, always enclose a stamped addressed envelope; this is only courteous and may speed things up.

A brief, precise letter, containing all the information required, is all that is needed. You should include a photocopy of all of your exam certificates, together with a CV (personal information and work history.) A photocopy of any written references, or addresses and phone numbers of oral references, might be very useful to your potential employer as a guide to your reliability. You must try to impress your potential employer, using all of your achievements as evidence of your suitability for the job. Always include where you heard of the job, for example in a newspaper, magazine or through personal contacts. If somebody let you know of the job, ask if you may use their name as an introduction; remember personal recommendations carry a lot of weight.

THE INTERVIEW

When you receive the letter asking you to come for an interview, you must reply promptly, acknowledging that you will be there.

You should dress smartly, remembering to take riding wear with you if your riding ability is to be assessed. When meeting your potential employer, you should be well mannered and polite. Do not ramble on and on. Check yourself to make sure that you are not, as nerves can sometimes make you unaware that you are doing this.

There are some very important points that you must establish from the start in order to achieve your aim of gaining fulfilling, lasting employment. A look at the conditions in the BHS recommended contract for working pupils (see p. 69) may also be of help when going for an interview.

1 *The hours that you will be expected to work:*
   Although with horses there are no 'normal' working hours, you have a right to know how long you will be expected to work for. Ask what days off you will be allowed and whether this is on a regular basis, being the same day each week or the same days every so often.

2 *Holidays:*
   The amount of holiday time to which you will be entitled will probably depend on how long you stay in the job, increasing each year. Whatever amount of holiday time you are allowed, you should find out whether it will be paid holiday or not.

3 *Accommodation:*
   If you are to 'live in' you must find out what accommodation is to be supplied. Accommodation can range from a bedroom in the main house, a caravan near the stables, or indeed the luxury of your own or shared accommodation in a small cottage or similar.
   Ask to have a look at the accommodation and to meet whoever you might be sharing with, if this is to be the case. You should also find out what accommodation is made if you are accompanying horses for 2- or 3-day shows.

4 *Exactly what does the job involve:*
   You will know roughly what type of work you will be expected to do from the type of place you are wishing to work in – riding

school, competition yard, stud work or racing; but it is as well to find out if any extra duties are involved such as housework or gardening, as this may not appeal to you.

5 *Wages*:
You must establish exactly how much you will be paid for the hours agreed; making sure it will be paid on the same day each week. Find out who is responsible for giving you your wages, as this might not be the employer him/herself.

6 *Promotional expectations and employment levels*:
The position you attain will of course depend on your own qualifications and ability. Try to find out if there will be chances for promotion, should you warrant it by becoming either better qualified or much more experienced, confident and knowledgeable. If you are wishing to start in a competition yard, find out whether you will have chances to ride with instruction, eventually being able to compete if you are good enough.

Now, because your interview was such a success, you will have got the job! A very satisfactory result for those of you who wish to start work straight away. If, however, you feel that you will not be able to get along with the employer or the other staff, or you are at all uneasy about your position, think very carefully before accepting the job.

7

Training establishments

There are many privately-run teaching centres throughout Britain. The majority offer courses leading to the BHS and/or ABRS and/or NPS qualifications (see pages 70–73). Most teach how to become an instructor, stud groom, yard manager or any other practical job that might be found within competitive or instructional yards. A few teach solely for the competitor.

If you decide upon a practical course of training to benefit your future prospects, you will need to find the right centre to suit you. Try to find a centre that has a wide range of courses to suit your individual requirements. You are more likely to succeed at a well-established centre with good, qualified instructors. This enables the equestrian industry to be built on a high standard of training, giving students experience over a wide variety of subjects. Good grooms are the backbone of the equestrian industry today. It is becoming more difficult to find trained, experienced grooms. Therefore grooms who have had the correct training and are prepared to stick with the job are in a better position to choose a career that will suit them.

DURATION OF COURSES

Courses depend entirely on what you require; that is to say, within the structure of a training establishment there should be a course length to suit you, giving you a good chance of passing the exam/s trained for, in the specified time. Depending on your previous experience, a course leading to the BHSAI might only be of 6 weeks intensive training. It is not a good idea to spend any less time training because you are being taught not only the subjects themselves but to put them across in a way that the examiner expects to hear.

It would certainly be more beneficial, if finances allow, to take your time and train on a course for 6, 8 or 12 months. This way you will be assured of having a thorough practical grounding, both with physical skills and theoretical study. Should it become apparent that you are advancing more quickly than expected, you should be able to go on and train for further exams.

If you are incorporating other studies with your equestrian exams, course lengths will differ. Your equestrian course may occupy only a couple of days a week, therefore it will obviously take longer to work through and understand the requirements of the exams for which you are studying. Some colleges work in conjunction with riding centres in the hope of equipping you with a wide variety of career possibilities.

You must be prepared to train for the first few years at an equestrian establishment or college that offers good career prospects for the future. Below are some examples of reputable training centres, to give you an idea of the sort of courses on offer, what to expect, and the sort of atmosphere you will be working in.

The training centres chosen (listed in alphabetical order) offer a variety of courses, including specialist training in certain fields or alternative training not specifically designed for instructors. Although they are all approved establishments, the list is not a guide to the elite few. They are all worth going to, but so are many more that are not listed. The surest way of finding a suitable place is to find the centre that offers you what you want. Then, if the centre is in your locality, seek more information regarding their courses. If it is not in your area, you must either be prepared to train away from home or to find the nearest centre that offers the facilities and courses to suit your needs. Most important of all, make sure that it has a good reputation and is approved by either the BHS or ABRS, as all of the centres listed in this book are.

DIRECTORY OF TRAINING CENTRES

Ayrshire Equitation Centre
Castlehill Stables, Hillfoot Road, Ayr. Tel: 0292 266267

The centre has accommodation for approximately fifty horses and ponies in enclosed yards. It is BHS, ABRS, STRA (Scottish Trekking & Riding Centre Association), P of B (Ponies of Britain) and RDA (Riding for the Disabled) approved, also being an examination centre for the STRA, a member of the British Driving Society and the highest approved examination centre in Ayrshire.

Short courses are arranged throughout the year to suit individual needs, with tuition being given for showjumping, cross-country, lungeing and stable management. Special one-day children's courses and holiday courses for both adults and children are available.

Various lengths of student courses are offered and to determine the type and length of course that will suit you, the centre organizes student assessments, from which they will give their recommendations for adults and children of all standards. All full-time student courses are grant-aided.

Bedgebury School Riding Centre
Bedgebury Park, Goudhurst, Cranbrook, Kent TN17 2SH. Tel: 0580 211602

Girls are accepted at Bedgebury School (which owns the riding centre) from the ages of 6 to 18 years. Girls in the sixth form can combine the BHS exams with A-level or commercial subjects.

Career training courses for the horse industry are also well catered for, the greater emphasis being towards the practical aspects. Training is provided towards the BHS exams up to the BHSI certificate. Approximately fifteen BHS exams are held at Bedgebury each year.

Catherston Stud and Equestrian Centre
Black Knoll House, Rhinefield Road, Brockenhurst, Hampshire SO42 7QE. Tel: 0590 22027

The Catherston Stud offers excellent prospects, enabling you to train for BHS exams, NPS exams (centre approved by both) and to learn to ride to a very high standard.

Excellent facilities are provided for those wishing to learn about stud work. These include three stable blocks, which contain a separate foaling unit with its own foaling boxes, feed-room, and sitting-up room for observation of foaling mares.

Top-class competition horses are prepared for all three disciplines and also produced for the show-ring. Horses are taken for breaking and schooling and private lessons are available for outside clients, with their own horses, by the resident trainer or instructors.

Courses offered include:

12 months	BHS Stages I, II, III and Preliminary Teaching Test combined with the NPS Stud Assistant's Examination.
6 months	BHS Stage III.
3 months	Stud management course (non-riding).
3 years	NPS Diploma course.

Training at a centre such as this is certainly likely to offer you a vast range of skills and experience in many different areas.

Eastern Equitation
Brickhouse Farm, Colne Engaine, Nr Colchester, Essex CO6 2HJ. Tel: Earls Colne 0787 222542

Eastern Equitation is approved by both the BHS and the ABRS. However, all career courses concentrate solely on the preparation for BHS examinations for Stages I and II.

The different methods of achieving the BHS qualifications are as fee-paying students, either full-time or part-time, where you can attend for anything from 2 hours per week to 4 full days per week. As a paying student you are offered complete flexibility, where training will be made to fit in with other commitments such as jobs or other studies.

As a BHS Stages student you can study for 2 hours at a time per week, either evenings or a morning class, whereby you will spend 1 hour riding and 1 hour engaged in practical or theory.

As a working pupil, which is mainly for school-leavers, you will be working in return for your tuition,where no money changes hands either way.

The centre is a YT managing agent for the scheme, accepting themselves about four students straight from school for either 1 or 2 years formal training. Other students applying for the scheme are placed in yards throughout Essex.

Harrogate Equestrian Centre
Brackenthwaite Lane, Burn Bridge, Harrogate, Yorkshire HG3 1PW. Tel: Harrogate 0423 871894

The Harrogate Equestrian Centre is BHS-approved to Stage IV, offering comprehensive training, primarily for those of you who wish to become riding teachers. You can be trained for any of the Pony Club, Riding Club or BHS exams.

Courses offered include:

(a) BHS HK & R Stages I, II, III, and PTT (minimum of 13 weeks for AI course)
(b) BHS intermediate and instructors' course
(c) Riding holiday course

(d) Pre-intermediate and instructors' course (minimum period of 4 weeks)
(e) Working students course

You can learn either on full fee-paying basis for courses *a–c*, or as a working student for courses *d* and *e*. For those of you who do not wish to become teachers, the training is devoted to the relevant needs of grooms and stable hands. The centre is ideal for those wishing to progress with their career training or competitive ambitions.

Leigh Equestrian Centre
Three Gates, Leigh, Sherborne, Dorset. Tel: Holnest 096 321 469

The centre is approved by the BHS and the ABRS and is a BHS examination centre, catering for children and adults of all abilities.
Courses offered:

(a) Short courses to suit the individual with tuition in all aspects of horsemanship including dressage, showjumping, cross-country, lungeing, instructional practice and stable management.
(b) Special 1-day courses for children.
(c) Holiday courses for families, adults and children of all abilities.
(d) Student courses of 3, 6, 9 and 12 months duration, providing training towards BHSAI and BHSII examinations.

The Limbury Stud
Hartpury, Gloucestershire. Tel: 045 270 268

The stud generally takes 16–18 year olds, who as well as receiving regular tuition in both riding and stable management, learn to mix with other people and cope with clients.

The stud is qualified to take NPS students for the stud exams, and also people wishing to train towards the BHS Stages I, II, and III (without the teaching).

Limes Farm Training Centre
Pay Street, Hawkinge, Folkestone, Kent CT18 7DZ.
Tel: 030389 2335

Limes Farm Training Centre is approved by both the BHS and the ABRS, offering a wide range of courses for anybody wishing to take the relevant exams.

Although it is a good place to train for a career, it also specializes in the training of students with their own horses wishing to improve in eventing, showjumping and dressage.

Grants are offered through the local education authorities and YT and Employment Training students are taken on, the aim being to make you employable at the end of your training. Alternatively, courses to gain required qualifications can be taken on a fee-paying or working-pupil basis.

As well as being able to take the courses set out below, specialist courses/clinics, competitions and riding for pleasure are also available.

Junior courses: courses for those wishing to take the Pony Club B, H or A tests are organized as well as regular showjumping courses.

Courses offered:

(a) 1 week crammer courses – BHSAI
(b) 2–6 week intensive course – BHS Stage examinations
(c) Set course for BHSAI or HK & R career students and BHSII career students
(d) Working pupil and YT course – BHS stages I, II and possibly III, Preliminary Teaching Test, Riding and Road Safety Test and ABRS Sssistant Grooms' Examination.

Loughton Manor Equestrian Centre

Redland Drive, Childs Way, Loughton, Milton Keynes, Bucks MK5 8AZ. Tel: 0908 666434

The centre is approved by the ABRS, the RDA and the BHS, also acting as an examination centre for them. It runs the two-year YT scheme 'Working with Horses' in association with North Bucks Equestrian Training, and is the only scheme in Buckinghamshire of its kind.

For career students there are courses leading to the ABRS Groom's Certificate and Diploma, the BHS Stages, the PTT and the BHSII. Activities such as summer riding holidays, own a pony for a day, evening showjumping club, hunter trials, a dressage show each summer and a one-day event for invited riding schools in the spring are all organized.

As well as the YT, you can train as a working pupil from between 12 and 15 months or as a fee-paying student from 1 to 12 months duration. The centre also offers a 2-year course leading to the GCSE in Horsemastership [see Chapter 1].

Northfield Riding Centre

Gorsey Lane, Bold, Nr St Helens, Merseyside WA9 4SW.
Tel: 0744 816075 (centre), 811175 (office)

Northfield is a BHS-approved training centre. Each student is trained to a high, individual standard. Northfield offers courses to suit individual needs and requirements. They offer BHS career courses up to the BHSII. This is in two parts comprising teaching and stage IV; either may be taken separately. Residential or non-residential courses are offered. You can have full- or part-time training, and they are active in both YT and working-pupil schemes.

Pittern Hill Stables Limited

Kineton, Warwick. Tel: 0926 640370

Pittern Hill Stables has much to offer students wishing to train for a career in many different areas of equestrianism. The centre is ABRS and BHS approved. Students' courses may be residential, non-residential or YT, but particular attention is given to students with individual needs and ambitions. Students are also sent from the Warwickshire Agricultural College to train for their BHS examinations, which form part of their chosen courses [see Chapter 8]. Evening classes are offered to all abilities. Teaching standards are high and students are able to take all ABRS tests up to Test 10 and BHS qualifications from Stage I up to BHSI.

Their teaching speciality is side-saddle, being the leading side-saddle school in the Midlands. They offer tuition for side-saddle grades up to Grade 4, which are set by the Side-Saddle Association.

The Talland School of Equitation

Siddington, Cirencester, Glos. Tel: Cirencester 0285 652318

Talland is one of the largest residential centres in the UK and has a fully qualified staff of two Fellows of the BHS, two BHSIs, supported by many BHSIIs and BHSAIs. The centre is approved by both the BHS and the ABRS and is an examination centre for the BHS for examinations up to and including the BHSII. Training is available to prepare for all examinations up to and including Fellowship level. Courses are of 16 weeks or 1 or more full years' duration.

All students are fee-paying. However, some local education authorities are prepared to assist applicants for grants to cover training fees. If necessary, English language lessons are available for overseas students.

Short courses can be arranged to suit the individual in dressage, cross-country, showjumping, side-saddle or for general-purpose equitation. Preparation courses, according to the season, are arranged for competitions, shows and hunting, and additional children's courses are staged for half-term and holidays.

Urchinwood Manor Equitation Centre
Congresbury, Bristol BS19 5AP. Tel: (Yatton) 0934 833248

The equitation centre is BHS, ABRS and NPS approved, offering a wide variety of career courses and competition training. Students may train for BHS stages I, II and III, BHSAI, BHSII, ABRS Groom's Diploma, Pony Club tests up to and including the A test and all Riding Club examinations.

Career courses can be taken on a full-time, part-time, fee-paying, working-pupil or YT basis. Alternatively, intensive training towards examination and competitions is available to suit all individual needs. Lessons are astride, but side-saddle instruction is an available choice.

Waterstock House Training Centre
Waterstock, Near Oxford, Oxfordshire OX9 1JS.
Tel: 084 47 616/460, or stable cottage 401

Waterstock House is geared for those who wish to train for a career or compete in competitive sports. Although it would appear that eventing is their specialist area, in fact they have produced riders at the highest level in showjumping, and to a lesser degree in dressage.

The main training programme is the career-pupil course of one year's duration. It provides a thorough grounding in basic horsemanship, giving a chance to gain all-round experience for a future with horses. Only a limited number of students are accepted each year, in order to give the best possible support.

Work in the centre's competition unit is done by personal agreement when requirements of the individual can be met. On successful completion of the career course you will be awarded a diploma, which will include a report on your progress.

Wellington Riding
Basingstoke Road, Heckfield, Hampshire RG27 0LJ.
Tel: 0734 326308

Wellington Riding offers full-time residential or non-residential courses leading towards the BHSAI, BHSII and BHSI certificates. Depending on ability and personal circumstances they run for 12 weeks, 24 weeks, 12 months, or 2 years YT courses. Except for the many overseas students who attend, the choice of courses is not made until students have attended an interview and been assessed. Plans are in place for transition to the new NVQs when the examining boards (BHS, ABRS and NPS) are ready.

Wellington Riding and Padworth College have also joined together to provide career students with a wider range of career possibilities (see Chapter 8).

Combined courses in stable management and equitation together with business or secretarial qualifications are provided by Wellington Riding and Padworth College. Two days each week are spent at Wellington, the aim being to achieve the preliminary teaching certificate, along with the other courses being studied for at Padworth.

The system is designed so that students progress from taking the BHS Stages I and II and the Riding and Road Safety Test, through to Stage III and the Preliminary Teaching Test, so leading to the BHSAI when ready. The length of courses range from 11 weeks to 2 years, depending on courses/subjects taken and the student's equestrian ability.

8
College courses

There are many colleges, some technical, some agricultural and horticultural, that provide courses for equestrian studies. These courses can be combined with vocational or non-vocational subjects. The courses provide more background knowledge than can be obtained from courses run by equestrian centres. The courses mostly range from National Levels 2 to 4 (see p. 74). The requirements for entry into these colleges vary, depending on the type of courses they run and which board sets the examinations. Colleges run within the state educational system cater for eventual employment, but it helps if they work in close contact with local employers for the equestrian trade.

If you have the necessary entry requirements, you could apply for a grant. You have to apply to your own local education authority (LEA) irrespective of which county you wish to train in. They will decide whether or not they consider you eligible, and indeed whether the course you are applying for is suitable not only for your needs but for the good of the employment situation in your area.

Anyone who has obtained a place on a full-time first degree course, a degree equivalent course, or a course that leads to an initial teaching qualification is elligible for a grant from their local education authority. Discretionary grants, depending on a number of factors, might be awarded for any non-designated course.

If you do not have the required number of GCSEs at the appropriate grades, you should seriously consider going to evening classes, or staying on at school, to try to get them. Nearly all colleges now require a good standard of academic training. Further study courses usually start in September at local colleges for people wishing to study or re-sit for examinations. Or there may be a chance for you to re-take exams early on in your chosen course.

Although full- or part-time courses are available in technical or agricultural colleges for all persons reaching the age of 16, subject to their entry requirements (some require one year's experience) you need not worry if you are applying when you are a few years older. There will be other people who have had to re-sit exams as well as you.

A worthwhile course should involve at least 1 year's hard work. You should be able to visit and work in different yards and establishments, where you will be expected to perform all duties in a different environment as confidently as if you were at your normal college. Some colleges have excellent on-site facilities, but it is just as important for you to gain experience in different areas of equestrianism. This is why you should be able to train both on and off site. All of the skills that you learn should be transferable, so that you can apply them to whatever part of the industry you eventually work in. It is as important to know how to fit a saddle correctly to a Shetland pony as it is to a £1 million racehorse.

PROFESSIONAL QUALIFICATIONS

Many colleges offer horse courses at different levels, and quite a few offer courses with just an element of horsemanship.

Most colleges use either the Business and Technician Education Council (BTEC) vocational courses or City and Guilds of London Institute/National Examinations Board (NEB) awards (see p. 99), with options to undertake either the BHS, ABRS, NPS, BDS exams or further academic qualifications.

Your choice of course is extremely important. You must decide upon the right course and then apply for it, even if it means travelling a long way and staying away from home. To make the right choice, you must understand at what level and for which part of the industry the course is aiming to train you.

■ BTEC examinations

The BTEC approves vocational courses in a wide range of subjects, including horse studies. The courses are not only aimed at those preparing for employment, but also for people in work. Courses can be studied in different ways, including full-time, day-release, evening, block-release, sandwich, and where appropriate open and distance learning courses. As well as degrees, the Council awards nationally-recognized qualifications in horse studies. The Council also offers pre-vocational courses in conjunction with the City and Guilds of London Institute.

For 14–16-year-olds there are foundation programmes, and for students aged 16+ there are courses leading to the Certificate of Pre-Vocational Education (CPVE).

The levels of BTEC qualifications are:

First Certificate (FC)   First Diploma (FD)
National Certificate (NC)   National Diploma (ND)
Higher National Certificate (HNC) Higher National Diploma (HND)

Continuing National   Continuing National
Certificate (CNC)   Diploma (CND)

■ *Entry requirements and lengths of courses*
The normal entry requirements and lengths for BTEC courses follow. You may also be admitted if you have other appropriate qualifications and/or relevant experience.

BTEC First Certificates and Diplomas
These are initial vocational qualifications for those who have chosen to embark on a career with horses. The courses are designed to develop essential skills and knowledge, and to provide a foundation for further study. You should have left school and be at least 16 years old. No formal examination passes are required, but you are expected to show evidence of ability to benefit from the course.

Length of course: certificate, 1 year part-time; diploma, 1 year full-time or 2 years part-time.

BTEC National Certificates and Diplomas
These are nationally-recognized qualifications for technicians or junior administrators.

You should be at least 16 years old and, for most courses, must hold a BTEC First Certificate/Diploma or four GCSE grade Cs or above, or a suitable alternative qualification such as a CPVE or a foundation programme with appropriate attainment.

Length of course: certificate, 2 years part-time; diploma, 2 years full-time, 3 years part-time or sandwich study.

BTEC Higher National Certificates and Diplomas
These are the qualifications for higher-technician, managerial and supervisory levels.

You should normally be at least 18 years old and hold an appropriate BTEC National Award, or an equivalent qualification, or at least one A-level pass plus appropriate supporting GCSEs. The actual requirements depend on the individual course, and a student entering with A levels may have to take additional bridging studies or a conversation course.

Length of course: certificate, 2 years part-time; diploma, 2 years full-time, 3 years part-time or sandwich study.

Continuing Education Certificates and Diplomas
These courses can be studied in various ways, and to be eligible you should be at least 21 and have appropriate experience.

■ *City and Guilds Awards*
In addition to conducting tests for the award of City and Guilds Certificates, the Institute provides services to other bodies such as the National Examinations Board. City and Guilds tests measure your knowledge and skills against nationally recognized standards. They are widely accepted throughout the industry. For most certificates there are no entry restrictions; however, each course lists any specific entry requirements.

Many City and Guilds qualifications have been conditionally accredited as constituent parts of NVQs.

DIRECTORY OF COLLEGES

Here is an outline of what courses technical and agricultural/horticultural colleges are offering throughout the UK. Where different colleges offer the same course, details of the course are given under 'Course Groups', beginning on p. 112. The detailed content of courses may vary to reflect local and regional needs.

Aberdeen College of Further Education
Kinellar, Aberdeen AB5 0TN

1 Preliminary Certificate in Horse Management (June–September).
   Qualifications attained BHS Stages I and II. Minimum age on entry 16.
2 Certificate in Horse Management (June–September).
   Qualifications attained BHS Stages III and PTT = BHSAI. Minimum age on entry 17.
3 Short Courses in Stable Management leading to NVQ/SVQ Level 1 or equivalent.
4 Day and evening classes in equitation and stable management.

Berkshire College of Agriculture
Hall Place, Burchetts Green, Maidenhead, Berkshire SL6 6QR

1 Equestrian Business Management (see Course Group 2b)
2 Equestrian and Business Studies (see Course Group 2h)
3 Day release course: one day per week leading to BHS examinations. There are no formal entry requirements although a riding assessment will be made. Qualifications available include: BHS Stage I, II and III, plus the opportunity to take the PTT – resulting in the BHSAI.
4 Short evening courses. These are of various lengths and types as appropriate.

Bicton College of Agriculture
East Budleigh, Budleigh Salterton, Devon EX9 7BY
The courses offered are progressive and follow on after either one or two years' Youth Training, which the college also provides.

1 National Certificate in the Management of Horses (NCMH) (see Course Group 1a). Opportunities to undertake the British Driving Society Groom and Carriage Driving Examinations. You will only be accepted if you already hold BHS stage II.
2 Advanced National Certificate (ANC) in Equine Business Management
   (see Course Group 3c).
3 Full-time courses are also offered leading to the Royal College of Veterinary Surgeons' qualification for Trainee Veterinary Nurses. There is also Youth Training in animal care.

Bishop Burton College of Agriculture
Bishop Burton, Beverley, North Humberside HU17 8QG

1 Higher National Diploma in Equine Management and Technology (see Course Group 3b) plus – you will have the opportunity of studying for the Diploma in Stud Management.
2 National Diploma in Equine and Business Studies
   (see Course Group 2f) plus – you will have the opportunity of taking the BHSAI early on in the course if you do not already hold it.
3 Advanced National Certificate in Equine Business Management
   (see Course Group 3c) plus – you will have the opportunity of studying for the Certificate in Stud Management.
4 National Certificate in the Management of Horses
   (see Course Group 1a) plus – when you reach the appropriate '

standard, you will be awarded a College Certificate in the Management of Horses; the British Red Cross or St John's Ambulance (or equivalent) First Aid Certificate; and either the BHSAI or appropriate RSA certificate in typewriting, depending on previous experience.

5 BTEC First Diploma in Horse Studies.
6 Youth Training in horse management.

Brackenhurst College
Southwell, Notts NG25 0QF

1 National Diploma in Horse Business Studies
   (see Course Group 2e).
2 BHSAI and Complimentary Studies
   (see Course Group 4h).
3 National Certificate in the Management of Horses
   (see Course Group 1a).
4 BHSII or BHSAI
   (see Course Group 4i).
5 National Certificate in Countryside Related Skills
   (see Course Group 2k).
6 Advanced National Certificate in Equine Business Studies
   (see Course Group 3c).

Brinsbury College
Brinsbury, North Heath, Pulborough, West Sussex

1 New Entrant Course in Equestrianism
   This is a 36-week course for those intending to join the equestrian industry. Leads to BHS Stages I and II depending on aptitude and previous experience. ABRS examinations and GCSEs are also offered.
2 Horsemaster
   This is a 36-week course for those who already hold BHS Stages I and II. You will work towards your BHSAI. ABRS Assistant Groom's and Groom's Diplomas are also offered.
3 Business Administration and Equestrian Studies
   This is a two-year course leading towards the National Certificate for farm secretaries and BHS examinations.

Day courses offered
4 Horsecare Training Scheme
   This is a YT course that is in line with the national preferred scheme for the horse industry.

5 Equine Health and Nutrition
   This course runs for 20 Wednesdays and is designed for those with horses in their care who wish to deepen their knowledge.
6 BHS Stages
   This course is an intensive programme for the dedicated student wishing to gain BHS qualifications.
7 GCSE Horsemastership (see Chapter 1)
   Those wishing to obtain this qualification may attend on a day-release basis (see Chapter 6)
8 Post-graduate Course in Equine Veterinary Nursing.
   This course is offered as a day release course of 20 weeks duration.

Evening courses offered
9 Horse Knowledge, Care and Riding
   Module 1: theory of equine management. Module 2: stable management practical. Module 3: theory of equitation and lungeing. All modules run for 10 evenings.

Short courses
Short courses are run for riding and road craft; cross-country fence construction; refresher preparation for BHS Stages I, II and III and PTT; and day-release lectures.
These courses are constructed to suit the requirements of groups and individuals.

Cambridgeshire College of Agriculture and Horticulture
Landbeach Road, Milton, Cambridge CB4 4DB

1 Cambridgeshire Certificate in Horse Husbandry and Secretarial Skills
   (see Course Group 1c) plus – options are also available for you to undertake rural tourism or rural business management modules, and additional studies in export and import marketing and commercial language development
2 National Certificate in the Management of Horses (NCMH)
   (see Course Group 1a).
3 Advanced National Certificate in Equine Business Management
   (see Course Group 3c) plus – This advanced national certificate is designed for those who wish to further their career opportunities within the equine industry by developing both practical skills and business acumen.

The course caters for people involved in the management of horses at livery, racing yards and studs; also for those people involved with teaching riding as a leisure pursuit. Special emphasis is given on this particular course to the requirements of teaching the disabled rider and suitable applicants may be able to gain the RDA instructors' certificate. Employment prospects are excellent both within the UK and beyond.

4   BTEC National Diploma in Horse Studies (Breeding and Stud Practice)
(see Course Group 2c). This is the first course of its type in the UK. It has been specifically designed at the request of the Thoroughbred industry. Students holding this diploma will have excellent career prospects, commencing with the position of stud groom – stud hand, head lad or unit supervisor. It is designed to serve you as well in Newmarket, Europe or throughout the world. The course is run jointly by the Cambridgeshire College and the Writtle College in Essex.

5   Full-time BHSAI Course.
This course is run in conjunction with Peterborough Regional College. You will attend the regional college for 2 years full-time study
(see Course Group 4b).

Cannington College
Cannington, Bridgewater, Somerset TA5 2LS

1   YT Horse Care and Management.
2   BTEC First Diploma in Horse Studies
(see Course Group 1g).
3   National Certificate in the Management of Horses (see Course Group 1a)

Carmarthenshire College of Technology and Art
Faculty of Agriculture, Pibwrlwyd Campus, Carmarthen, Dyfed SA31 2NH

1   BTEC First Diploma in Business and Equine Studies
(see Course Group 1g).
2   National Certificate in the Management of Horses
(see Course Group 1a).
3   Advanced National Certificate in Equine Business Management
(see Course Group 3c).

Chippenham Technical College
Cocklebury Road, Chippenham, Wiltshire SN15 3QD

1 BTEC National Diploma in Equestrian Studies
   (see Course Group 2d).
2 Horse Management and Training (BHSAI)
   (see Course Group 4a).
3 BHSAI and NCA in farm secretarial or home economic studies
   (see Course Group 4c).

Clynllifon College of Agriculture
Ffordd Clynnog, Caernarfon, Gwynedd LL54 5DU

1 National Certificate in the Management of Horses
   (see Course Group 1a).
2 Stage III and PTT (BHSAI).
3 A varied range of short courses on aspects of horse management.

Dewsbury College
Halifax Road, Dewsbury, West Yorkshire WF13 2AS

1 BTEC National Diploma in Equestrian Studies
   (see Course Group 2d).

Duchy College of Agriculture and Horticulture
East Cornwall Centre, Stoke Climsland, Callington, Cornwall PL17 8PB

1 National Certificate in the Management of Horses [NCMH]
   (see Course Group 1a).
2 BTEC Diploma in Equine Business Management
   (see Course Group 2b).
3 Office Studies [Equestrian] Course
   (see Course Group 1f).

Lancashire College of Agriculture and Horticulture
Myerscough Hall, Bilsborrow, Preston, Lancashire PR3 ORY

1 National Certificate in the Management of Horses
   (see Course Group 1a).
2 BTEC First Diploma in Horse Studies
   (see Course Group 1g).

3 BTEC National Diploma in Equine Studies
(see Course Group 2d).

Lincolnshire College of Agriculture and Horticulture
Caythorpe Court, Caythorpe, Grantham, Lincs NG32 3EP

1 First Diploma in Horse and Stable Management
(see Course Group 1g).
2 National Diploma in Equine Studies with Agriculture
(see Course Group 2j).
3 National Certificate in the Management of Horses
(see Course Group 1a) plus – you should normally have a minimum of 2 years' working experience with horses since leaving school and should be at least 17 years old. This may be in the form of a YT or First Diploma course prior to entry, although this is not essential.
4 Advanced National Certificate in Equine Business Management
(see Course Group 3c) plus – you should be 18 years of age and hold the NCMH.

Moulton College
Moulton, Northampton NN3 1RR

1 Management of your horse or pony. This is a 10-week evening course, held for 2-hour sessions each Tuesday.
2 Small animal and horse care.
3 National Certificate in the Management of Horses
(see Course Group 1a).
4 BTEC First Diploma in Horse Studies
(see Course Group 1g).
5 Advanced National Certificate in Equine Business Management
(see Course Group 3c).
6 Horse Management and BHSAI with AS, GCSE and/or business subjects
(see Course Group 4c).
7 Horse Management and BHSAI with A level and/or business subjects
(see Course Group 4d).
8 Advanced Horse Management and BHSII
(see Course Group 4e).

Norfolk College of Agriculture and Horticulture
Easton, Norwich NR9 5DX

1 BTEC First Diploma in Business and Finance, with equestrian option
   (see Course Group 1g).
2 BTEC National Diploma in Business and Finance, with equestrian option
   (see Course Group 2g).
3 Horse Owners' Knowledge, Care and Riding Courses.
   These are modular courses on a day-release basis leading to BHS qualifications up to BHSAI.

Norfolk College of Arts and Technology
Tennyson Avenue, King's Lynn PE30 2QW

BHSAI course
(see Course Group 4j). Many of the BHS examinations are catered for, such as the BHS Stages I – III HK & R and the preliminary teachers certificate. It is possible to combine these with A Level, GCSE, secretarial or business studies. There are also opportunities for part-time and full-time courses as well as YT and Employment Training. Provisions are also made for training with riders who have disabilities. Training and assessment is given for NVQ Levels 1 and 2. Open learning packages are also available for beginners to advanced, with tutor support.

North Lincolnshire College
Cathedral Street, Lincoln LN2 5HQ

Equitation (BHSAI) with supporting studies
(see Course Group 4n) plus – those of you who already hold the BHS HK & R Stage II may complete the course in 1 year of study as opposed to 2. In this instance, a package of relevant supporting studies will be specifically prepared to meet your own needs and abilities.

Oatridge Agricultural College
Ecclesmachan, Broxburn, West Lothian EH52 6NH

1 Full-time Certificate in Horse Management
   (see Course Group 1a).

2 Full-time Advanced Certificate in Horse Management.
All students have the opportunity of obtaining a SCOTVEC National Certificate in each course taken, which lists all modules successfully achieved. Equitation and teaching practice is aimed at achieving instructional qualifications to the levels of BHSAI and BHSII.
3 YT Horse Care.
The preferred scheme for horse care follows nationally agreed guidelines to meet the needs of both trainees and industry.

Padworth College
Nr Reading, Berkshire RG7 4NR

1 Equitation and Stable Management with English as a Foreign Language
(see Course Group 4k).
2 Equitation and Stable Management with Secretarial Studies
(see Course Group 4j).
3 Equitation and Stable Management with Business Studies
(see Course Group 4m).

Pembrokeshire College
Haverfordwest, Dyfed SA61 1SZ

1 National Certificate in the Management of Horses
(see Course Group 1a).
2 Horse Studies and Office/Secretarial Skills (combined certificate)
BHS Stages I and II, RSA certificates (office skills) will be examinations catered for. One year full-time.

Pencoed College
Pencoed, Bridgend, Mid Glamorgan CF35 5GL

1 YT Horse Studies (BTEC First Certificate)
2 National Certificate in the Management of Horses
(see Course Group 1a).
3 BTEC First Diploma in Horse Studies
(see Course Group 1g).
4 Advanced Course in Equine Studies.

Peterborough Regional College
Park Crescent, Peterborough PE1 4DZ

1   BHSAI and associated studies
    (see Course Group 4b).
2   Equine Studies and Stable Management
    Length: Evening classes, 2 hours a week for two terms.
    Leads to: Arrangements can be made to take the BHS Stage exams,
    but you will need to arrange your own riding and practical man-
    agement tuition.
3   YT for skills in the horse industry.

Plumpton Agricultural College
Nr Lewes, East Sussex BN7 3AE

   1 Preliminary Certificate in Horse Management.
   2 National Certificate in the Management of Horses
     (see Course Group 1a).
   3 Advanced National Certificate in Equine Business Management
     (see Course Group 3c).

Part-time courses offered:
   4 Horse Knowledge and Care.
   5 Horse Care and Riding Instruction – stages 1 and 2.
   6 Preparation for Work.
   7 Equine Business Management.
   8 Stable Management.
   9 Various saturday practicals.
  10 Introduction to Driving.
  11 BHS Preliminary Teaching Test.
  12 BHS Intermediate Teaching Test.

Sparsholt College
Hampshire, Sparsholt, Winchester SO21 2NF

Full-time BTEC First Diploma in Horse Studies
(see Course Group 1g).

Staffordshire College of Agriculture
Rodbaston, Penkridge, Stafford ST19 5PH

1   National Certificate in the Management of Horses
    (see Course Group 1a).
2   BTEC First Diploma in Equine Studies
    (see Course Group 1g).

Stockton-Billingham Technical College
The Causeway, Billingham, Cleveland TS23 2DB

1 Horse Management and Training
   (see Course Group 4f).
2 Horse Management and Training Part-time.
   Students for this course in-fill into the full-time courses. It is available for up to 21 hours per week with a commitment for 2 years.
3 Basic Horse and Pony Care.
   This course is designed for those buying a horse in the near future, or those with little experience in looking after a horse or pony. It runs on Thursday evenings for 10 weeks.
4 General Horse and Pony Care.
   This is a follow-on course for those who have completed the basic course, whose needs are more advanced. It also runs on Thursday evenings for 10 weeks.

Thomond College
Plassey Technological Park, Limerick

1 Certificate in Equestrian Studies.
   One year full-time. A leaving certificate or equivalent and five subjects at grade D (OL) are required for entry. The qualification gained is the National Council for Educational Awards Certificate.
2 BSc degree in Equestrian Studies.
   Four years full-time including one year's industrial experience. Six subjects, two at grade C (HL) are required for entry. The qualification gained is a BSc degree in Equestrian Studies.

Tresham College
St Mary's Road, Kettering, Northants NN15 7BS

1 BHSAI with Combined Studies
   (see Course Group 4g).
2 Part-time study for mature students is also available.

University College of Wales
Old College, King Street, Aberystwyth SY23 2AX

Degree of MSc in Equine Studies.
If interested in taking the course, which makes extensive use of the services of distinguished contributors from the veterinary and equine

research world, you will be expected to complete a dissertation on some aspect of equine science. Although most students have first degrees of a scientific flavour, applicants from holders of arts/social science degrees are by no means discouraged, while mature non-graduates with appropriate qualifications and experience are also welcome to apply. Since the course concentrates on the biological aspects of equines, extensive equestrian experience is not a prerequisite. Those wishing to pursue the BHSAI concurrently with the MSc may do so by arrangement.

Walford College of Agriculture
Baschurch, Shrewsbury SY4 2HL

National Certificate in the Management of Horses
(see Course Group 1a).

Warwickshire College for Equine Studies, Agriculture and Horticulture
Moreton Morrell, Warwickshire CV35 9BL

1 National Certificate in the Management of Horses
   (see Course Group 1a) plus – training towards the BHSAI is offered. BHS Stages I and II or equivalent and one year's practical work are entry requirements for this college.
2 National Diploma in Horse Studies (Equine and Business Management)
   (see Course Group 2a).
3 Advanced National Certificate in Equine Business Management
   (see Course Group 3d) plus – as well as the ANCEBM, you will also be prepared for taking either the BHSII or the Warwickshire Certificate in the Development of the Performance Horse and the BHS HK & C Stage IV. If you already hold the NCMH or a similar qualification from another college you will be awarded the Warwickshire Diploma in Equestrian Studies on completion of the course. For this option the college accepts a BHS Stage III HK & C as an entry requirement.
4 Higher National Diploma in Horse Studies (Management and Technology)
   This course is run in conjunction with the Coventry Polytechnic. A split year is organized for industrial placements. At the end of the course you will be qualified as a yard or business manager, and following further industrial experience could expect to secure a

managerial or executive position
(see Course Group 3b).

5 Young Grooms Training Scheme
Up to 2 years for school-leavers on YT. This course is generally only available to those living in Warwickshire or the West Midlands.

6 Equine Studies Modular Degree
The degree and the honours degree are unique to this college. The course lasts four years, including a sandwich year out, and is modular so students have a choice of study subjects. As with the HND, entry is via PCAS and is listed under Coventry Polytechnic.

Welsh Agricultural College
Llanbadarn Fawr, Aberystwyth SY23 3AL

Higher National Diploma in Horse Studies
(see Course Group 3b).

West Oxfordshire College
Holloway Road, Witney, Oxon

The courses are geared totally for the science and practice of stud and stable husbandry (Thoroughbred) and as such incorporate:

1 National Certificate in the Management of Horses (Thoroughbred)
(see Course Groups 1a and 1b).
2 National Diploma in the Management of Thoroughbred Horses
(see Course Group 2i).
3 BTEC Higher National Diploma in Stud and Stable Administration
(see Course Group 3d).

Students from the stud and stable husbandry courses are employed worldwide throughout the Thoroughbred industry.

Worcester College of Agriculture
Hindlip, Worcester WR3 8SS

1 The Certificate in Stud and Stable Husbandry
(see Course Group 1d).
2 The Racing Industry Course
(see Course Group 1e).

Writtle Agricultural College
Chelmsford, Essex CM1 3RR

1 Higher National Diploma in Agriculture (Equine Studies option) (see Course Group 3a).
2 Diploma in Horse Studies (Breeding & Stud Practice) (see Course Group 2c).

COURSE GROUPS

This is a list of courses offered by the colleges. It will show you which courses are open to you and what qualification you can hope to attain. Once you have decided on the college and course to suit you, apply to the college for more information.

■ *Course Group 1*

(a) National Certificate in the Management of Horses (NCMH)

Aims: To provide a basic understanding and appreciation of the fundamental principles of horse management and associated farming industries.

Qualifications gained: On completion of the course you will take the examination leading to the NCMH. According to individual needs and abilities, you may also be prepared throughout the year for other examinations. These may include (depending on the college), BHS Stages I, II, III, IV, BHSAI, ABRS Groom's Diploma, Pony Club H and A Tests. The level of the course is NVQ Level 2.

(b) National Certificate in the Science and Practice of Stud and Stable Husbandry (preparation for Thoroughbred industry only)

Aims: To prepare students for suitable employment in a range of occupations associated with horses.

Qualifications gained: NCMH (Thoroughbred); RSA office practice examinations (students are entered according to ability).

(c) Cambridgeshire Certificate in Horse Husbandry and Secretarial Skills

Aims: To produce people trained to a high level of competence and adaptable to an ever-changing work environment.

Qualifications gained: UEI Phases 1 and 2; ABRS Assistant Groom's Diploma; ABRS Groom's Diploma; BHS Stages I, II, III, BHSAI; RSA 1 and 2 in keyboarding – accounts – office practice – word processing.

(d) The Certificate in Stud and Stable Husbandry

Aims: To offer training and qualifications for those who wish to obtain sound, basic, technical, practically-based experience for a career working with horses and ponies. Its block design provides the ideal opportunity for those already working in equine establishments to obtain such training. There is no riding involved, thus the study can be kept intensive.

(e) The Racing Industry Course

Aims: This course is designed for trainers, assistant trainers and senior yard staff. It provides the technical training needed to meet the changing requirements dictated by scientific research and development. It aims to provide instruction on the equine husbandry facets of horses in training. It is directed at the many people who are working at training establishments and perhaps are skilled in matters associated with breaking, riding and training routines, but who require more background and technical information.

(f) Office Studies [Equestrian] Course

Qualifications gained: After 1 year you will enter for the relevant RSA qualifications for your office studies. You will also take your equestrian studies exams after 1 year. The level of progress and competence gained will determine what BHS qualifications will be attained, taking into consideration the level of qualification on entry to the course. It is anticipated that most students entering with no BHS qualifications will attain BHS Stages I and II during their study.

(g) BTEC First Diploma in Business and Equine Studies

Qualifications gained: BHS Stages I and II.

■ *Course Group 2*

The main aims of the courses in this group are to provide the student with an insight and detailed knowledge of science and practice in the horse industry together with an understanding of business management. To give students the potential of running their own yard or being a responsible person on the larger equestrian establishments. Or alternatively, the opportunity to go on to higher education.

(a) National Diploma in Horse Studies

Qualifications gained: BHS HK & C Stage IV; with further experience the Stable Managers' Certificate [BHS (SM)].

(b) **BTEC National Diploma in Equine Business Management**

Qualifications gained: BTEC in Business Studies; BHS Stages I, II, III, IV, BHSAI, etc.

(c) **National Diploma in Horse Studies (Breeding and Stud Practice)**

Qualifications gained: BTEC in Horse Studies (Breeding & Stud Practice)

(d) **BTEC National Diploma in Equestrian Studies**

Qualifications gained: BTEC ND, BHSAI, with opportunities at some colleges to take the National Proficiency Test in Tractor Driving and First Aid Certificate.

(e) **BTEC National Diploma in Horse Business Studies**

Qualifications gained: BTEC National Diploma in business studies (Horse Option); BHSAI.

(f) **National Diploma in Equine and Business Studies**

Qualifications gained: Diploma in Equine Business Studies; BTEC ND in Business & Finance (Equine Options); BHSII; British Red Cross or St John's Ambulance First Aid Certificate.

(g) **BTEC National Diploma in Business Studies (Equestrian Option)**

Qualifications gained: BTEC in Business Studies; BHSAI.

(h) **Equestrian and Business Studies Course**

Qualifications gained: BTEC in Business Studies; BHSAI.

(i) **National Diploma in the Management of Thoroughbred Horses**

Qualifications gained: BTEC in Agriculture (Management of Thoroughbred horses); College certificate in the Science and Practice of Stud and Stable Husbandry.

(j) **National Diploma in Equine Studies with Agriculture**

Qualification gained: BHSAI; proficiency tests in computers and agricultural skills.

(k) **NC in Countryside Related Skills**

Length: One year, full time. Apply to Brackenhurst College for more details.

■ *Course Group 3*

The courses in this group are more advanced, aiming to produce skilled practical people to become competent managers, run their own enterprises or take up responsible positions in associated activities.

(a) Higher National Diploma in Agriculture (Equine Studies)

Qualifications gained: BTEC HND in Agriculture (Equine Studies option)

(b) Higher National Diploma in Horse Studies (Management and Technology)

Qualifications gained: opportunities for suitable candidates to undertake the BHS HK & C Stage IV, BHS (SM) after further experience; BHSII; BHSI; ABRS and NPS examinations.

(c) Advanced National Certificate in Equine Business Management (ANCEBM)

Qualifications gained: ANCEBM; BHS Stages up to Stage IV; BHSII.

(d) Higher National Diploma in Business and Finance (Stud and Stable Administration)

■ *Course Group 4*

The courses in this group are designed to prepare students for a wide variety of careers in the horse world, but in particular emphasis will be placed upon training students to become effective teachers of riding. However, it has become increasingly important for riding instructors and those intending to make careers with horses to have a sound educational and business background. Therefore, preparation for public examinations in academic subjects will complement the instructors' course.

(a) Horse Management and Training (BHSAI)

Complementary studies available: GCSE and GCE A levels, BTEC ND in Business Studies (Equestrian option).
Qualifications gained: BHSAI; GCSE, commercial or secretarial examinations appropriate to individual needs.

(b) BHSAI and associated studies

Complementary studies available: BTEC HNC in Business and Finance. BTEC ND in Business and Finance (Equestrian options). GCE

A level. GCSE. Secretarial studies. Some combination of subject areas may be possible.

Qualification gained: Year 1: BHS Stages I and II; BHS Road Safety, First Aid Certificate; academic subjects according to course. Year 2: BHS Stage III; BHS Preliminary Teaching Test – BHSAI; academic subjects according to course.

(c) Horse Management and BHSAI with AS, GCSE and/or business subjects

Complementary studies available: A range of AS, GCSE level and/or agricultural, horticultural and secretarial studies can be selected.

Qualification gained: College certificate in horse management; BHSAI; AS, GCSE, level or agriculture, horticulture and secretarial qualifications as selected.

(d) Horse Management and BHSAI with A Level and/or business subjects.

Complementary studies available: Wide range of A level, GCSE and/or business and secretarial studies can be selected.

Qualification gained: College Certificate in Horse Management; BHSAI; A level and/or GCSE subjects; other vocational qualifications – business and secretarial studies.

(e) Advanced Horse Management and BHSII

Qualification gained: College Certificate in Advanced Horse Management; BHSII.

(f) Horse Management and Training Course

Complementary studies available: Secretarial Subjects, GCSEs and GCE A-level certificates.

Qualification gained: BHSAI; academic subjects as selected.

(g) BHSAI with combined studies

Complementary studies available: Choice of over thirty GCSE and A-level subjects, combined with secretarial studies.

Qualifications gained: BHSAI; selected studies.

(h) BHSAI and complementary studies

Complementary studies available: Secretarial skills or A-levels or leisure and recreation or rural enterprise.

Qualifications gained: BHSAI; RSA Stages 1 and 2 or BHSAI; A-levels, two or three from wide range, or BHSAI; City & Guilds Leisure and Recreation 481.

(i) BHSII or BHSAI

Complementary studies available: None, although the course provides a business and financial element appropriate to the needs of a small business.

Qualifications gained: BHSII or BHSAI

(j) BHSAI course

Complementary studies available: GCSEs, GCE A-levels and business subjects.

Qualifications gained: BHSAI; selected GCSEs or GCE A-levels; RSA examinations.

(k) Equitation and Stable Management with English as a Foreign Language

Complementary studies available: Intensive English as a foreign language.

Qualifications gained: Depending on ability, students are encouraged to take BHS Stages I and II, and wherever possible to progress to Stage III and the PTT, thus culminating in the award of the BHSAI. Students are prepared in their English studies for Cambridge First Certificate, Cambridge Proficiency, JMB, Oxford, RSA, ARELS and TOEFL.

(l) Equitation and Stable Management with Secretarial Studies

Complementary studies available: Shorthand/speedwriting; typewriting; wordprocessing; Bookkeeping; office practice.

Qualifications gained: BHSAI; relevant Pitman and RSA examinations.

(m) Equitation and Stable Management with Business Studies

Complementary studies available: Business related skills; information processing; keyboarding or typewriting with one option from marketing, finance, advertising, industrial relations or wordprocessing.

Qualifications gained: BHSAI; BTEC Certificates in above business studies.

(n) Equitation (BHSAI) with supporting studies

Complementary studies available: Full range of GCSEs, GCE A-levels and BTEC qualifications plus ENFEC shorthand and typing certificates.

Qualifications gained: BHSAI; as selected from above.

(o) BHSAI and NCA in farm secretarial or home economics studies

Complementary studies available: National Certificate in Agriculture providing opportunities to study in farm secretarial or home economics.

Qualifications gained: BHSAI; NCA.

Appendix:
Organizations and addresses

The British Horse Society (BHS)
British Equestrian Centre, Stoneleigh, Kenilworth, Warwickshire CV8 2LR.
Tel: 0203 696697

The British Horse Society aims to improve the standards of care of horses and ponies, as well as encouraging the use of horses and ponies, and promoting the interests of horse and pony breeders. It is also interested in improving standards of riding.

Through its committees it cares for horses and all riders. It has a welfare committee that works in close contact with the RSPCA and police, investigating complaints and resolving problems of abuse and misuse.

Through its network of Regional and County Officers it aims to preserve existing rights-of-way and help to open up safe riding routes in the countryside. It has campaigned for several years, and still does, to raise the level of riding and road safety.

The society trains and examines those who are making careers with horses as grooms, competitors, yard managers, trainers or instructors. Training is recommendd at BHS-approved establishments. The society's exams are not aimed specifically at stud work or racing.

The Riding Clubs
c/o British Horse Society, British Equestrian Centre, Stoneleigh, Kenilworth CV8 2LR. Tel: 0203 696697

All Affiliated Riding Clubs are affiliated to the British Horse Society. If you become a member of such a club, you will be able to take part in showjumping, eventing, dressage, training and examinations to a recognized and approved standard.

They aim to encourage riding as a sport, to promote good fellowship among riders, to improve and maintain the standard of riding and horsemanship and to keep bridle paths open and maintain facilities for riding.

Training organized by clubs covers all levels and all disciplines.

The Pony Club

British Equestrian Centre, Stoneleigh, Kenilworth, Warwickshire CV8 2LR.

Tel: 0203 696697

The Pony Club is for all young riders who share a love of horses and ponies. It teaches young people how to ride correctly and how to care for their ponies. Although not all members of the Pony Club own ponies, they do all ride.

As well as encouraging young people to ride better and teaching them how to look after horses and ponies properly, it aims to show them how to gain the maximum fun out of riding.

Local branches organize many activities where youngsters can take part and enjoy many different competitions and championships. The big dream of every pony clubber is to take part in the Prince Philip Cup Mounted Games Championship which takes place at Wembley.

British Field Sports Society (BFSS)

59 Kennington Road, London SE1 7PZ. Tel: 071-928 4742

The British Field Sports Society promotes understanding and responsibility in attitudes to country sports. It fights to safeguard a heritage of British country sports, such as fishing, hunting, shooting, hare coursing and falconry. The society is kept in touch with local and individual problems through a network of regional and local secretaries. Its parliamentary committee fights unnecessary controls and bans, and campaigns for national and international agreements on the conservation of wildlife.

British Show Jumping Association (BSJA)

British Equestrian Centre, Stoneleigh, Kenilworth, Warwickshire CV8 2LR.

Tel: 0203 696516

The BSJA is the governing body for showjumping in the UK. The association's purpose is to improve and maintain the standard of showjumping, encouraging members of all standards and at all levels to enjoy fair competition over safe and attractive courses.

The association runs classes to cater for all abilities, from the less courageous or younger horse and rider through to top-class international competition as seen at Olympia, Hickstead, The Royal International and the Horse of the Year Show.

The British Driving Society (BDS)

27 Dugard Place, Barford, Nr Warwick CV35 8DX.

Tel: 0926 624420

The British Driving Society is the parent body for all driving enthusiasts in Britain, and the liaison link with drivers throughout the world. It aims to encourage and assist those interested in the driving of horses and ponies. The society has proficiency tests in four grades to enable members to confirm their driving ability. Everyone, whether they drive or not, is welcome to join the society and take part in its activities.

Association of British Riding Schools (ABRS)
Old Brewery Yard, Penzance, Cornwall TR18 2LS.
Tel: 0736 69440

The Association aims to raise the standard of instruction, horsemanship, and the welfare of horses and ponies in riding establishments. It wishes to assure the public that if they choose an ABRS approved establishment they will be able to obtain sound riding instruction, which is well presented and correct in content.

The Assistant Groom's Certificate and the Groom's Diploma provide a guideline for the employer to judge a groom's competence. In addition to these examinations, the association runs the weekly-rider equitation, stable management and side-saddle tests in order to help employers, to give an interest to clients, and to provide a programme from which instructors can work at a practical level.

The National Pony Society (NPS)
Brook House, 25 High Street, Alton, Hants GU34 1AW.
Tel: 0420 88333

The NPS encourages the breeding, registration and improvement of riding ponies and mountain and moorland ponies, and fosters the welfare of ponies in general.

The NPS Diploma Examination Scheme provides practical and technical training in all branches of pony management at inspected, approved establishments. The examination demands a high standard of efficiency and knowledge. The holder of this qualification is widely recognized and highly regarded throughout the industry.

Riding for the Disabled Association (RDA)
Avenue 'R', National Agricultural Centre, Kenilworth, Warwickshire CV8 2LR.
Tel: 0203 696510

The RDA provides pleasure in the form of riding or driving for people with disabilities. Although many riders who have disabilities are children, adults are also catered for. All helpers, instructors and physiotherapists are volunteers. Training for helpers is given at local and regional level. Anyone who has enthusiasm, dedication and a willingness to work with riders with disabilities is most welcome to join their local member groups.

It is possible for riders with disabilities to undertake a series of proficiency tests that provide a guide to their progress, although this does of course depend on the nature of the rider's disability and how regularly they ride. The essential requirement is that riding should give pleasure and fun to all who take part in it.

The Farriers Registration Council
P.O. Box 49, East of England Showground, Peterborough PE2 0GU.
Tel: 0733 234451

Details of careers in farriery and of the Student-Apprenticeship Scheme may be obtained from the Farriers Registration Council.

More information may also be supplied by either: The Registrar, The Worshipful Company of Farriers, 3 Hamilton Road, Cockfosters, Barnet, Herts EN4 9EU. Tel: 081 449 5491; National Organizer, National Association of Farriers, Blacksmiths & Agricultural Engineers, Avenue 'R', 7th Street, N.A.C., Stoneleigh, Kenilworh, Warwickshire. Tel: 0203 696595; Head of Engineering Department, Hereford Technical College, Folly Lane, Hereford HR1 1LS. Tel: 0432 352235

Metropolitan Police
New Scotland Yard, Broadway, London SW1H 0BG

When applying to the Metropolitan Police for information regarding careers in the Mounted Police Force, address your enquiries to the Directorate of Public Affairs. Although you will have to want a career as a *normal officer* first, they will supply you with information regarding training for both mounted officers and the horses.

Royal College of Veterinary Surgeons (RCVS)
32 Belgrave Square, London SW1X 8QP.
Tel: 071 235 4971

The RCVS publishers booklets entitled *A Career as a Veterinary Surgeon* and *Veterinary Nursing* which are available from the RCVS at a small cost.

The Thoroughbred Breeders' Association (TBA)
Stanstead House, The Avenue, Newmarket, Suffolk.
Tel: 0638 665621

The purpose of the association is to represent all British breeders, whether they are breeding on a large or small scale, both for the Flat and National Hunt.

The TBA will send out literature on courses available throughout the country that are suited to those wishing to pursue a career in the bloodstock industry. They will also supply a list of TBA members who are willing to employ students.

Racing and Equestrian Section

Agricultural and Allied Workers National Trade Group (TGWU), Transport House, Smith Square, Westminster, London SW1P 3JB. Tel: 071 828 7788

The Racing & Equestrian Section organizes the largest trade union for the horse industry. It is working to improve wages and conditions within the industry. Once you have left school and decided on a career with horses, you are eligible to become a member of the Racing & Equestrian Section and enjoy the Union's many benefits, as well as protection from exploitation.

The Jockey Club

42 Portman Square, London W1H 0EN. Tel: 071 486 4921

The Jockey Club will advise on all matters within the racing industry and will supply information regarding careers in horseracing.

The National Trainers' Federation

42 Portman Square, London W1H 0AP. Tel: 071 935 2055

The National Trainers' Federation gives help in placing boys and girls with employers.

The British Racing School

Snailwell Road, Newmarket, Suffolk.

The school offers courses to train stable staff each year, and will also provide advanced courses for potential jockeys and work riders. Full details of the courses can be obtained from Major M.F.T. Griffiths at the above address.

Northern Racing School

Rossington Hall, Great North Road, Doncaster DN11 0HN. Tel: 0302 865462

This school also offers courses of up to 2 years duration and is open to both sexes. Further details should be obtained from Mr J. Gale at the above address.

Weatherby's
Sanders Road, Wellingborough, Northamptonshire NN8 4BX.
Tel: 0933 440077

Weatherby's provide racing's civil service, being responsible for the day-to-day running of the sport. They employ administrative staff and in addition to secretarial and clerical staff, they also employ staff for their extensive computer operations.
   Other employers of administrative staff within the racing industry are:
   The Horserace Betting Levy Board, 52 Grosvenor Gardens, London SW1W 0AU.
   The Horserace Totaliser Board, Tote House, 74 Upper Richmond Road, London SW15

Saddlers' Company (The Worshipful Company of Saddlers)
Saddlers' Hall, Gutter Lane, London EC2V 6BR.
Tel: 071 726 8661/6

The Saddlers' Company will supply you with information regarding the pattern of training to become a saddler. The traditional method of entering the trade, by being apprenticed to a master saddler, still applies to the industry.
   Organizations which run training courses in this craft are:
   The Cordwainers Technical College, Mare Street, Hackney, London E8 3RE. Tel: 071 985 0273;
   Walsall Leather Training Centre, 56/57 Wisemore, Walsall. Tel: 0922 721153;
   Cambridge & District Saddlery Courses, Pinford End Farm House, Pinford End, Hawstead, Bury St Edmunds, Suffolk IP29 5NU. Tel: 0284 86213.

The Chartered Society of Physiotherapy
14 Bedford Row, London WC1R 4ED.
Tel: 071 242 1941

The society will give you details of a career in physiotherapy and will put you in touch with the Secretary of the Association of Chartered Physiotherapists in Animal Therapy.

Bibliography

ABRS, *ABRS Official Handbook*

Andrist, Fredrich, *Mares, Foals and Foaling*

Basil BHSI, Julie, *After the AI*

BHS, *Instructors Handbook*

BHS, *Levels of Horse Care and Management Books One and Two*

BHS, *Riding and Road Safety Manual*

BHS, *The Manual of Horsemanship*

Britton, Vanessa, *Riding for the Disabled*

Canning, Joanne, *Revision Notes I, II, III*

Canning, Joanne, *Revision Notes on Prelim Teaching*

Canning, Joanne, *Revision Notes on Stage IV*

French, J. *BHSAI Course Companion*

Green, Carol, *Stable Management Explained*

Harris, Charles, *The Fundamentals of Riding*

Houghton Brown, J. and Powell-Smith, V., *Horse and Stable Management*

Houghton Brown, J. and Powell-Smith, V., *Horse Business Management*

Kane, Jeanne and Waltman, Lisa, *The Events Groom's Handbook*

Mortimer, M. *BHSI Stable Managers Study Notes*

Mortimer, M. *Horse Owner's Handbook*

Mortimer, M. *Notes on Preparation for BHS Horse Knowledge and Riding Stages I and II*

Mortimer, M. *Notes on Preparation for BHSAI Certificate*

Mortimer, M. *Notes on Preparation for BHS Intermediate Certificate*

Mortimer, M. *Notes on Preparation for BHS Instructor's Certificate*

Mortimer, M. *Notes on Careers Working With Horses*

Museler, William, *Riding Logic*

Rose, Mary, FBHS, *The Horsemaster's Notebook*

Sivewright, Molly, *Thinking Riding*

Index